the sleeping
GIANT

The Awakening of the Self-Employed Entrepreneur

Ken McElroy

the sleeping
GIANT

The Awakening of the Self-Employed Entrepreneur

Ken McElroy

KYLEKADE
PRESS

Published by: Kylekade Press
Printed in the United States of America

ISBN-13:   978-0-9829108-0-1

The Sleeping Giant is available for special promotions and premiums.
For details contact Kylekade Press at:
8553 E. San Alberto
Scottsdale, AZ 85258
480-998-5400
info@thesleepinggiant.com

Or visit www.thesleepinggiant.com

Cover photo by Kelli Leslie
Jacket design by PCI Publishing Group

First Edition: January 2011

10 9 8 7 6 5 4 3 2 1

Library of Congress Cataloging-in-Publication Data

McElroy, Ken
   The sleeping giant: the awakening of the self-employed entrepreneur / Ken McElroy – 1st ed.

To my father, Ronald Charles McElroy,
rest in peace,
who gave me the greatest gift:
he believed in me.

**Fall seven times,
stand up eight.**

- Japanese Proverb

ACKNOWLEDGEMENTS

This author gratefully acknowledges Jake Johnson, Mona Gambetta, Sue Hesse, and Heasley and Partners for their assistance throughout this project as well as the 20 Authors in this book for believing in this venture, their time and efforts and agreeing to donate the profits to charity. To both my forums in EO and YPO, for helping with the vision for this book and for sharing experiences that will create legacy. And to Robert and Kim Kiyosaki for giving this average student the opportunity to see the impact that can be made with just a little vision and effort.

The net profits from this book
will fund charitable ventures.

CONTENTS

FOREWORD
by Robert Kiyosaki

For the better part of my adult life, I've made it my mission to teach people to be financially intelligent and financially free. This is why I'm an entrepreneur in financial education. My book, *Rich Dad Poor Dad*, was centered on the financial wisdom I gained from my rich dad, my best friend's dad. I've transferred my rich dad's lessons to readers via simple stories from the book and my financial education board game, CASHFLOW, which translates my rich dad's lessons into actions. The game allows the participants to make mistakes and learn from them using play money before they invest real money. As you know, humans learn by making mistakes. Both written and physical lessons are essential to anyone who wants to become an entrepreneur and investor.

I've known Ken for close to a decade. He is, in my opinion, the smartest real estate entrepreneur in the world. His thoughts and actions are far ahead of his time. Who else talks about infinite returns on investments and practices what he preaches? As a business partner in several of Ken's ventures, I value Ken as one of my advisors, a speaker at my seminars, and an author. Sharing his wisdom via the Rich Dad brand, Ken has evolved into a premier educational entrepreneur. Over the years, he has also become a close friend and a trusted advisor. We've made millions together by being generous rather than being greedy.

One of the things I appreciate most about Ken is his passion for life and for others. Ken is enthusiastic about being an entrepreneur and sharing what he knows. As most of us know, the more you give, the more you receive—and Ken is a person who loves to give. Ken also knows that the best way to solve the unemployment problem is by inspiring more people to become entrepreneurs, because only entrepreneurs create real jobs. This is why Ken is the driving force behind this book. He wants other entrepreneurs to share what they know.

Many people are blessed with success and wisdom, but fail to give back. One of the reasons I've made Ken a trusted advisor is because his mission is in line with my own: to elevate the financial well-being of humanity. And like me, Ken knows that teaching others about entrepreneurship is key in helping others become financially free and lead happier, healthier, and more fulfilled lives.

What Ken has done with this book is nothing short of amazing. He's brought together twenty men and women who have incredible stories of success in business and investing to share. These stories are powerful, and you can't help thinking differently about the world after reading them. These are stories made on the hard battlefield of business, earned at great cost. These stories are like the stories from my rich dad. They are stories about real life in business, rather than business theories from school. Now they're yours—and they're priceless.

If you're looking for a better way to live, this book will open your eyes to the importance of entrepreneurship, both for you and for our world. Don't just browse these stories. Digest them.

And at the end, don't just read these stories. Make your own.

Robert Kiyosaki

Introduction
The Awakening of the Sleeping Giant

Opportunity is abundant, even in the harshest of economic times. I've been a self-employed entrepreneur most of my life, but never before have I seen such massive opportunity as exists today. With the ever-increasingly connected world, businesses can be created virtually overnight using a portable computer and the Internet. The only thing missing is you and an idea.

Right now, whether you realize it or not, there's a Sleeping Giant getting ready to awaken, a massive community of people who understand that the world, and how it does business, is changing, and that the only way to survive is to create opportunity rather than to wait for it to come to them. Over 100 million people represent the Sleeping Giant, and they'll fight for employment survival.

Let's look at the facts about the Sleeping Giant:

> Over 15 million people are unemployed at this writing.

> People are living longer, and most don't have the financial means to retire.

> Life expectancy is now at 85. Yet, only 1 in 10 Americans is financially prepared for retirement.

> The average savings of a 50-year-old is only $2,500, and about 17,000 people turn 50 every day.

Of the 74 million Baby Boomers (born between 1946 and 1964), most aren't financially ready for retirement, and 68 percent (over 50 million) plan on continuing to work after retirement, according to a Gallup poll. As these folks view their retirement options, it should be no surprise that they are also starting small businesses faster than any other age group.

The Baby Boomers' kids represent a large, up-and-coming segment of the U.S. population. Generation X (born between 1965 and 1980) represents a total of 66 million people, and Millennials (born between 1981 and 2000) represent another

86 million people. These two groups include a total of 152 million people.

As most kids *do*, the Baby Boomers' kids do the exact opposite of their parents, and in this case, it seems that is a very good idea. Not only will most of these 152 million kids receive little or no inheritance, but it also appears they'll be taking on some serious government debt that will be in the trillions. And ultimately, these same kids may even be in a position to later have to care for the very parents who raised them.

As my friend Robert Kiyosaki, author of *Rich Dad Poor Dad,* says, it seems that the old adage of "Get a safe, secure job and save for the long term" didn't really work for most of the Baby Boomers, and it's definitely not working for their kids.

The New American Dream

Entrepreneurship and self-employment are becoming the new American dream. According to *Money/U.S. News and World Report*, half of all college graduates now believe that self-employment is more secure than a full-time job, and colleges and universities have responded—over 80 percent of higher-learning institutions now offer courses on entrepreneurship.

According to a CNN/*USA Today*/Gallup poll, 72 percent of eighteen- to twenty-nine-year-olds want to start their own businesses. You can see the survey at *http://www.gallup.com/poll/15832/Majority-Americans-Want-Start-Own-Business.aspx*. These future self-employed entrepreneurs are part of the Sleeping Giant. Current and future employees can and will turn to self-survival because they've witnessed this past decade as a loss of wealth, financial mismanagement, and lack of loyalty by many employers. The solution will be to take matters in their own hands.

The world is entering a very exciting time because The Sleeping Giant will create jobs and stimulate the economy. These new and existing businesses will need support, mentorship, and funding sources, and will revolutionize and "awaken" millions of people over the next decade, which in turn will create job growth and instill personal freedom in those who must or wish to take the journey.

You can be part of this movement. All you need is an idea and a support network. If you take this step and are successful, you'll no longer be a statistic of the crashing economy. You won't have to rely on anyone—except yourself—to prosper, and you'll be in complete control of your future.

At this moment, you still have a choice. You can continue to slumber and get stomped on by the Sleeping Giant when it awakens. Or you can wake up and join this revolutionary wave of personal freedom.

This book contains twenty stories by self-employed entrepreneurs. Each one started with nothing but an idea, and most had no experience or money. Some of these businesses were strategic; others were started out of desperation. As you'll discover, each entrepreneur's story is a completely unique journey, and the lessons each author shares are invaluable.

One thing each author has in common is that during their journey to becoming self-employed, they all sought mentorship by joining an organization called Entrepreneurs' Organization (www.eonetwork.org), a non-profit organization that helps global entrepreneurs become better business and community leaders. I've been a member since 1999. EO has also been a huge influence and support structure in my own entrepreneurial journey. I'm deeply indebted to them and the relationships I've formed through the organization. Profits from this book will be used to fund educational initiatives sponsored by EO for new and existing businesses.

The Way Things Were

When I was growing up, you could always tell who was in the upper-middle class. They were well-dressed in suits and had a confidence about them. They drove nice cars and had nice houses. They had it all. These were hard-working, well-educated people who'd worked their way up the corporate ladder. They took pride in their positions as vice presidents or presidents of companies they'd worked for most of their lives. They were the perfect example of where hard work and loyalty could get you.

That was a different time for America. It was marked by steady-as-she-goes business growth and frugal, budget-conscious families.

Most of all, it was marked by loyalty.

I'd say that loyalty was the defining characteristic of my parents', and probably your parents', generation. There was an expectation that if you worked hard for a company, the company would take care of you. That's why companies gave pensions, promoted from within, bought company cars, and handed out gold watches. The perks were meant to reward, not just retain, good, hard-working talent.

Back then, people didn't jump from company to company like they do now. Many people spent much of, if not their whole, lives working for the same employer, punching in their 9-to-5, having BBQs and going to church on the weekends, trading from a Ford to a Buick, from a three-bedroom house to a four-bedroom house, saving for the kid's college fund, and paying down their debt. It was a pretty predictable and measurable path to prosperity and security.

I think we all know those days are long gone. And they're not coming back.

The World Has Changed

As of 2008, the last survey by the Bureau of Labor Statistics (BLS), the average time an employee spends at one particular job is 4.1 years. That's down over 80 percent from the 1950s. Nobody nowadays goes into a job anymore thinking, "This is it. This is what I'm going to do with my life. I'm going to work for this company until I retire." Instead, we go in thinking, "I should get enough experience and contacts in the next couple years to be able to move up to a better position and get a higher salary at another company....I hope I don't get laid off first."

Why do we think like that?

I think the answer is pretty simple: The world has changed. Somewhere along the line, as profits increased exponentially, as labor overseas became cheaper and cheaper, and as unfettered expansion became their focus, companies shrugged off that troublesome burden of loyalty to employees and replaced it with an insatiable loyalty to shareholders. And as companies became more and more focused on cutting costs and increasing productivity, you, the employee, became overworked, underpaid, and, let's face it, replaceable.

That's why wages are stagnant, barely keeping up with inflation, and why you haven't seen that raise you "deserve." The economic crisis hasn't helped. In fact, 2009 was the worst year on record for wage growth, which averaged just 1.8 percent, and wage growth in 2010 is expected to be the second worst on record at 2.5 percent. To add insult to injury, the top 10 to 15 percent of workers captured most of those gains. In other words, your boss is getting a raise—and you aren't.

Why am I mentioning all of this? Because these statistics validate what you already know either consciously or subconsciously—you're not going to be rewarded for being loyal to your company. Instead, you're going to fall further and further behind the economy as the years go by. And so, you're forced to look for a higher paying job every few years. Everyone does it, and there's really no end in sight. The old economy is broken, employers have pushed their employees too far, and the employees have revolted. They've become free agents looking for the best contract they can find.

A Snapshot of Today

Here's the deal. You don't need to be an economist to understand that jobs are hard to come by and that the economy is in trouble.

I want you to stop for a moment—I mean, really stop, right now—and think about the devastating and unprecedented economic crisis we've been through and are, as I write this, still experiencing. You've never been through anything like this in your life. Here are some shocking statistics:

> Over 15 million people are unemployed in the U.S.—more than the entire population of New York City—nearly 10 percent of the entire workforce.

> The U.S. government has racked up record debts of nearly a trillion dollars in bailouts and loans—more than all previous bailouts *combined*.

> Real estate lost $3.4 trillion in wealth—roughly $30,300 per household.

> The stock market lost $7.4 trillion in wealth—around $66,200 per household.

And things aren't going to get better. In Richard Duncan's 2003 book, *The Dollar Crisis*, he predicted that the U.S. property bubble would trigger a global recession, which we are obviously experiencing now. And in Duncan's new book, *The Corruption of Capitalism*, he contends that the United States government will be at least $17 trillion in debt in 2019. Most of America's industries are not globally competitive, and the private sector has grown so dependent on debt that it can no longer service. The country is dependent on credit growth as the driver of economic progress, has lost much of its manufacturing base, and continues to de-industrialize because its wage rates are up to 40 times higher than those of low-wage countries.

These trillion-dollar annual deficits will need to be funded for the next decade just to keep the United States from collapsing into a severe depression. But this funding will do nothing to restore the economy's long-term viability. In 2020, the U.S. economy will still be dependent on debt, and even more trillion-dollar budget deficits will be needed to support it in the years that follow.

If you take a careful, honest look at these numbers, the gravity of this crisis will begin set in. It's hard to take in. The numbers are so big that they seem nearly impossible to wrap your mind around. But each one of those numbers represents real people whose lives have been or will be destroyed—some of whom have taken their own lives. Those numbers represent real families losing all they've worked for. They represent real desperation and tragedy.

Maybe they even represent you.

New Economy, New Opportunity

The good news is that you don't have to stay shackled to the old economy. There's an entire movement of people taking matters into their own hands and bravely forging the new economy—an emerging self-employed entrepreneur, the New Business Class—and you're just in time to be part of it.

The new economy will provide an entire new set of opportunities and level the playing field for those paying attention. In the process, these opportunities will create the largest transfer of wealth in our lifetime. It doesn't matter who you are or how old you are. You can participate in the new economy. You can thrive while others cling to an old and dying system.

Maybe you're a Baby Boomer who's worked your whole life honing your craft and building your career, only to watch it all melt away in the last several years. With the market tanking, your retirement account is down, the equity in your house is gone, and your job is at risk. Maybe you're scared and uncertain about what to do. This book is for you.

Maybe you're a young, up-and-coming businessperson staring at the future with despair. You've seen your parents work their fingers to the bone, only to watch it all come crashing down. You feel intuitively there has to be a better way. This book is also for you.

Or maybe you're an entrepreneur who's taken the leap and built your own business, but this economy has hit you hard. Numbers are down, and you're desperately looking for a way to shake things up and gain some traction. You need a little inspiration. This book is for you, too.

The first step is to truly believe and understand that *the old way of doing business and work isn't the answer*. Only then will you be able to fully join the New Business Class.

So, what is the New Business Class? What is this Sleeping Giant?

It's the overwhelming majority of up-and-coming workers who intuitively understand that the system is broken—and rather than try and fix it, it's better to just move on.

It's the huge wave of Baby Boomers who've lost their jobs or who are facing retirement but don't have the financial resources to retire, but who do have resolve. They're people who bring a lifetime of talent and experience to the table, and who know they can do something for themselves for a change.

And it's the small, pioneering class of people who call themselves the self-employed, small-business owners or entrepreneurs who've taken the leap and started their own businesses, and who know the freedom and thrill that comes with building something from the ground up.

The members of the New Business Class understand that the world and the way business is done have fundamentally changed. And they know that change is the only constant in a culture where technology has flattened the playing field and innovation occurs at the speed of light. Those who have joined the New Business Class don't fear change—they embrace it and profit from it.

This is your time to make a change. This is your opportunity to become a part of the New Business Class and take your future into your own hands. Besides, you don't really have a choice—things are changing with or without you. The rules of the game have changed, and unless you adjust the way you think about money—and how you make it—you'll be at a serious disadvantage in this new economy.

It's time for you to become a self-employed entrepreneur.

The Heartbeat of America

Self-employed entrepreneurs and small-business owners are the heart of our economy and are responsible for almost everything that's positive about it. Small businesses represent the majority of all employers and have ***always*** been in control of the fate of the U.S. economy. According to the Ewing Marion Kauffman Foundation (www.kauffmann.org), one of the largest foundations in the world dedicated to entrepreneurship, in the last twenty-five years, nearly all *net* job growth for the United States was from firms less than five years old. Here are a few more reasons entrepreneurs and small businesses are such a force to be reckoned with:

> Entrepreneurs have been responsible for 67 percent of the inventions and 95 percent of the radical innovations made since World War II, according to the Public Forum Institute.

> Less than 1 percent of entrepreneurs surveyed came from extremely rich or extremely poor backgrounds, according to The Kauffman Foundation.

> More than half of the companies on the 2009 Forbes 500 were launched in a recession or a bear market.

> Job creation from start-up companies proves to be less volatile.

> 2009 represented the highest entrepreneurial rate in fourteen years.

The heartbeat of America isn't a Chevy truck after all—it's entrepreneurs. An increase in the New Business Class will result in an increase in employment, wealth, and quality of life for all Americans and the world. When the Sleeping Giant fully awakes, the world will be fundamentally changed—for the better.

This awakening is long overdue and is happening out of necessity. It embraces all ages, all races, and all religions; it doesn't discriminate. The New Business Class is a movement of displaced workers who are in a unique position of being unemployed or even employed but unsure of their future. They understand that the rules of the game have changed, and they're taking control of their futures and their finances through new business creation. In the process, they're helping solve this financial crisis, business by business, city by city, state by state, and country by country.

This book is intended to help nudge, assist, and possibly even motivate you to believe that you too can create your own future—and to act on that belief. The future of your country—and yes, even the world—will be determined by you, one business at a time. It's not too late. It's only just beginning.

You Have the Power

When companies gave up their loyalty, they also gave up their power. In the old economy, you didn't switch jobs even if you wanted to. Why? You'd lose all the hard-earned perks and your pension. You'd have to start all over again. Nobody wanted to do that. In return, companies retained their employees and their skills because leaving was a too-much-to-lose proposition.

But in the new economy, you really don't have much to lose. You can always roll your retirement savings plan over—or kill it, which is my advice. You can always find a better position, doing more of what you love, with more flexibility, at a better-positioned company, making more money. And there's really not a thing your present employer can do about it.

And what some people are discovering is that they not only can move freely between companies, leveraging their skills and talents to attain better positions with better pay, but they can also become their own boss. They can find the balance they're looking for in life, successfully combining work and play, becoming masters of their time, talent, and future. They can take their passions, skills, talents, motivations, energy, and time, and build something that is entirely their own. They can leave behind the old economy of employee and employer and march bravely into the new economy of entrepreneurship.

They can join the ranks of the New Business Class.

Bye-Bye Middle Class, Hello Business Class

People used to aspire to be middle class. They wanted to have a family with two-and-a-half kids, a house with a white picket fence, and a nice car. That was the good life. You'd really arrived. A few brave souls dreamed of more. Not just more material possessions but also of a future of freedom, doing work they were fully invested in and controlling their own destinies. But for the most part, people aspired to be in the middle class. It was safe, secure, and afforded unprecedented luxury for the average person.

Today, the middle class is shrinking, and soon it will be all but gone. Today, people don't aspire to thrive; they aspire to survive. The U.S. Department of Commerce and Economics and Statistics Administration released a report in

January 2010 titled "Middle Class in America." That report drew the following conclusion: "Many families, particularly those with less income, will find attaining a middle class lifestyle difficult if not impossible. Areas with high housing costs can make even higher-income families feel pinched. Lack of employer-provided health insurance can confront a family with bankrupting health costs. And unforeseen expenses can ruin even the best-laid budget plans."

In July 2010, a *Yahoo! Finance* article showed the following statistics:

> Eighty-three percent of all U.S. stocks
> are in the hands of 1 percent of the people.
>
> Sixty-one percent of all Americans live
> paycheck to paycheck.
>
> In 2010, 21 percent of all children
> are living below the poverty line

Why is it that everything is getting more expensive, yet inflation is reported to be so low? Intuitively, we know that the cost of living is rising rapidly. And we also know that the dollar is losing value. The U.S. saving rates for banks are at an all-time low, and if you continue to deposit money to your savings account, you're actually being paid less in bank interest than the reported inflation rate. In other words, if you're saving your hard-earned dollars in the bank, then those dollars will buy you less in the future.

In the meantime, salaries have either fallen or remained stagnant. No business could survive such steep increases in expenses with no measurable increase in income—and the middle class can't, either. The American Dream through traditional employment is quickly becoming unattainable.

Even worse is the prospect of retirement for the middle class. A *USA Today* article titled "Middle-Class Americans' Retirement at Risk" states, "Of all the threats to the American middle-class standard of living, from stagnating incomes to piles of consumer debt, perhaps the least understood and among the most serious is the looming crisis in retirement. Traditional pension plans are disappearing in the private sector. Workers aren't saving enough in their voluntary retirement savings plan 401(k) accounts. Longer life spans are stretching savings even thinner. Social Security remains under stress. Furthermore, all that was going on before retirement plans lost $2 trillion in the recent stock market dive."

The article gives some even more alarming statistics. Nearly half of American workers have less than $50,000 saved for retirement, and over 20 percent of workers say they have no savings of any kind. If you couple those statistics with the fact that only around 10 percent of Americans have a company-provided pension plan, that government entitlement programs like Social Security and Medicare are sprinting toward insolvency, and that a majority of employees are banking on the stock market for retirement, you can see that there's a retirement crisis looming.

As Seth Godin says in his book *Linchpin*, "Suddenly, quite suddenly in the scheme of things, it seems like the obedient worker bought into a sucker's deal." Your employer isn't going to save you. You must save yourself. You have to say bye-bye to the middle-class dream and embrace the New Business Class future.

The good news is that you can. And you're not alone.

This Sleeping Giant is larger than you'd ever imagine.

The Baby Boomers' Spoiled Kids

One segment of the Sleeping Giant is the largest generation since the Baby Boomers, and it's just reaching working age. This generation is called a variety of names—the Echo Boomers, Generation Y, Millennials, and Generation Next, to name a few—but whatever you call them, they're big (all combined, 152 million strong), young, adaptable, and a mystery to corporate America.

There are scores of articles, books, and blogs on how to deal with these kids. They've got this pesky independent streak. They don't like to work long hours. They want to play as much as they work. And they don't seem to be motivated by money. What's a middle manager to do?

Now, get this: According to *Newsweek,* 65 percent of the Echo Boomers want to start their own businesses. Entrepreneurship is the norm, not the exception, for Echo Boomers. Consider this quote from a *USA Today* article titled "Gen Y makes a mark and their imprint is entrepreneurship": "Experts say these children of the baby-boom generation, also known as Gen Y or Echo Boomers, are taking to heart a desire for the kind of work-life balance their parents didn't have. They see being their own boss as a way to resolve the conflict. So now they're pressing ahead with new products or services or finding a new twist on old-style careers. They're at the leading edge of a trend toward entrepreneurship that has bubbled for decades and now, thanks in large part to technology, is starting to surge." That's what I mean by the Sleeping Giant.

Think about it. If even 25 percent of these kids become entrepreneurs, that's over 30 million new businesses—and a radically altered economy. The Sleeping Giant. The New Business Class. The future.

Baby Boomers—The New Mid-Life Crisis

Maybe by this point in the book, you're thinking, "Ken, this is all well and good, sounds great even, but I'm not a reckless twenty-something with nothing to lose. I'm a grown up with grown-up responsibilities. I have a family and a mortgage. I can't possibly step out on my own, even if I want to."

Yes, you can. There are thousands upon thousands of Baby Boomers just like you who are and will be part of the Sleeping Giant. These are men and women who understand that they have much more to accomplish—and the skills and experience to not only strike out on their own, but also to succeed.

In fact, one of the fastest growing segments of entrepreneurs is the 55 to 64 age group, according to the Ewing Marion Kauffman Foundation. Between 2008 and 2009, the number of entrepreneurs in that group grew to two million—an increase of 5 percent. And the number of entrepreneurs aged 65 and older grew by a whopping 30 percent!

I'm here to tell you that The New Business Class isn't a one-trick pony. It's not just a young person's game. It's for everyone. In fact, I'd say that the New Business Class needs the Baby Boomers to survive. Young energy can only get you so far. Experience and wisdom are must-have commodities.

And you can be a part of this movement. You can be a part of the New Business Class. You can join the Sleeping Giant. You can take control of your own future. You can find security and freedom by becoming an entrepreneur. I'm giving you permission. Because sometimes permission is all we need.

If you're feeling hesitant about what I'm saying, here's why: You've been conditioned into thinking that true responsibility is going to school, getting a good job, saving your money, buying a nice house, and doing what you're told. You've been trained that way ever since you were a little kid, dutifully getting up when the bell rang at school, moving to the next class, sitting down when the bell rang again, going home, doing your homework, and getting up to do it all over again the next day. You were trained to not speak unless called upon, to stay on pace with everyone else, to never let your brilliance shine or outshine others.

This training may have even carried into your college days, where you went from class to class, filling out forms, taking prerequisites you never needed or have used since, plodding dutifully towards graduation while wondering what you were going to do with your life.

And it continues now that you're working. Punching in and out, fifty hours a week, plowing through hundreds of mundane e-mails and spreadsheets, and watching others make more money, experience more success, and live the life that you want to live—the life of freedom.

You've been trained to look at the world as one of scarcity. In that world, you're replaceable—a dime a dozen. In that world, you can lose your job at any minute. Your savings can be wiped out at the whim of the market. And you must tightly clutch what you have before someone else takes it.

But that world doesn't exist anymore. That's the old economy.

The new economy is one of abundance. In the new economy, anyone can join the New Business Class. Anyone can be an entrepreneur.

The Changing Mindset

As Seth Godin points out, "Today, the means of production = a laptop computer with Internet connectivity. Three thousand dollars buys a worker an entire factory." The order has been disrupted, and corporate America is losing power to incorporate entrepreneurs.

What do I mean by incorporate entrepreneurs? A defining trait of those who belong to the New Business Class is that they know the value of collaboration and a team. Those in the New Business Class have been trained to work on teams from a young age. And they're not afraid to share. They see the world as one of opportunity and abundance. They understand that the more you exchange and partner, the more successful everyone becomes.

As such, the old system of highly tiered, corporate juggernauts is on its way to extinction. That system isn't sustainable, given the rise of the Sleeping Giant. Instead, it's being replaced with an incorporate system—a system of loosely connected entrepreneurs who come together for various projects and then go their own way to team up with other workers on yet new projects. This trend is identified in books like *Noded: The Untouchable Business* by Andreas Carlsson and Jaan Orvet, which defines the Noded concept as "A group of individuals, often but not necessarily geographically distant, that come together to form temporary or recurring project teams. Unlike 'distributed teams,' Noded teams work for a wide range of clients and any member of a Noded team can take the lead to bring in work, manage work and choose their team members."

Why would people choose to work in such a way? Because they understand that it's riskier to rely on a company or someone else for their financial future than to rely on themselves. They don't believe that they'll see Social Security or Medicare when they retire, they know that they'll probably inherit government debt, they know that a company pension won't be there as a safety net and that many of their parents are broke, and they certainly understand that working sixty hours a week to barely stay ahead isn't worth it. So they're taking things into their own hands. Is it risky? Sure. But it's riskier to be an employee.

Here's the amazing thing the Sleeping Giant understands: The world has changed and only those that adapt will survive. Those who cling nostalgically to the old economy will be wiped out.

What It Takes

In this book, you'll find stories of entrepreneur pioneers. This is a gift. If you truly want to join the New Business Class, you're sure to find the motivation and the knowledge you need to be successful just by reading these stories. What you'll also find is that there's no cookie-cutter formula for being an entrepreneur. Contrary to popular belief, there is no standard personality type or age group necessary for being a successful entrepreneur.

Before we move on to those stories, I want to share some of the qualities and groundwork it takes to be a successful entrepreneur. Because inspiration, while important, is only half the battle. This part of the introduction will help you understand what it takes to be a successful entrepreneur, and it will also point you to some of the stories in the book that highlight the points I'm making.

Diff'rent Strokes

If you're old like me, you might remember the old television show "Diff'rent

Strokes." The show was about a rich white businessman on Park Avenue who adopts two African American boys from a poor Harlem neighborhood after their mother, who worked for the man, dies. The boys go from rags to riches literally overnight. Hilarity ensues.

The truth is that the show explored some very real racial and economic tensions. Part of the theme song went like this: "Everybody's got a special kind of story/Everybody finds a way to shine/It don't matter that you got not a lot/So what, they'll have theirs, and you'll have yours, and I'll have mine/ And together we'll be fine/Because it

> *Shawn Thomas' story,*
> *"The Journey Is the Success,"*
> *is a must-read if you think*
> *your background is holding*
> *you back from taking hold*
> *of your future.*

takes, Diff'rent Strokes to move the world/Yes it does/It takes, Diff'rent Strokes to move the world." It might be a theme song for a silly show, but those are profound truths, no?

Now, before you hit me with, "What you talkin' about, Kenneth?," let's think about this song for a second. If you want to be part of the New Business Class, if you want to be part of the Sleeping Giant, it doesn't matter who you are, where you come from, or what you have. You can find a way to succeed. The world needs you, as unique as you are, to engage it with your particular brilliance, personality, and talents.

The reality is that a number of factors go into how you'll approach becoming an entrepreneur. Let's take a look at some of them.

Personality

Some people are natural born extraverts and adventurers, while others are naturally shy and introspective. No matter if you're the life of the party or the quiet wallflower, you can be successful as an entrepreneur. The world needs different personalities. If we were all the same, nothing would get done. And each personality type has advantages (and disadvantages) that others don't.

For instance, if you're shy and introspective, chances are you're probably also very thoughtful. You're able to think through choices and their implications, to consider the feelings and motives of others, and to persuade others to follow you. Crazy extraverts don't always have this ability. They tend to rush into a situation and then use their sheer force of personality and energy to make it work. In the process, they may leave behind some carnage, both in terms of people and business.

The crazy extravert can rally people to follow through personality and energy. People follow crazy extraverts, often blindly, because they're so convincingly confident about where they're going (even if they don't really know for sure!). They tend to be optimists who say, "I can make this work. I don't know how, but I'll figure it out as we go." Quiet introverts can't do this and will often fail if they try. They tend to be more pessimistic and may overanalyze. And sometimes their fear of conflict means that they don't push people toward success like they should.

Yet, both personality types can be successful entrepreneurs if they recognize their strengths and weaknesses, and surround themselves with a team of people who can supplement their shortcomings and enhance their strengths.

Life-Stage

No matter what your personality, the simple truth is that it's not always just about you. Business is definitely a team sport, and understanding this will make you more successful. If you are open to this very simple fact, the world will be your playground. When I started my business, I made the mistake of thinking mostly about myself and what I wanted. I worked

> *Jim Small's story "Higher Purpose" is a must-read and an important reminder that nothing is more important than your family—and why building a great business is the best way to care for them.*

way too much and neglected my family. I wasn't initially as good a dad or husband as I could've been. And many entrepreneurs fall into this trap of overworking at their company but under-working at home. If you're open-minded, you learn as you go.

Thankfully, early in my career, I joined organizations like Entrepreneurs' Organization (EO) and Young Presidents Organization (YPO) and met some very wise men and women who taught me the importance of balancing both work and home life. I made changes that not only made me a much better dad and husband, but also a much better boss and entrepreneur.

For some of you, this may not be much of a consideration. You might be single and able to focus only on yourself and your business. If so, you'll be more apt to take bigger risks and to put in longer hours. Or you might be a spouse and a parent with much more to think about than just yourself. Even if you're completely comfortable with huge risk, are you comfortable with risking your family and their well-being? These are hard questions everybody needs to consider before thinking of going into business.

It's self-evident, but I'm going to say it anyway: The more you have, the more you have to lose. If you're a risk-taking extravert, you better stop for a second and consider the cost of what you want to do and whether there's a better way to arrive at the same end. If you're a risk-adverse introvert, you should stop and consider whether you're letting the fear of risk hold you back from making some great moves for you, your business, and your family.

Friends

The old saying, "Birds of a feather flock together," is true. Sometimes the most important thing you can do to change your mindset and move toward fulfilling your passions and dreams is to shed some of your old contacts who pull you down. If you have friends who say, "You can't do that" or, "That sounds too risky" or, "You don't have any good ideas," you might need to say, "Thanks for all the years of friendship, but I've got to move on." Because the reality is that if your friends can't support you—within reason—they're not really friends. Part of changing your mindset is surrounding yourself with people who have the mindset you want. And part of becoming successful is being around people who are more successful than you.

You see this all the time in professional sports. How many stories have you heard about a young athlete who has the potential of a great future? The world is handed to him on a plate, but he's dragged down by old friends and acquaintances.

Over the years, I've been privileged to mentor and advise many famous sports figures on finances and investing. Many of these young players have no financial knowledge, and suddenly they're rich beyond their wildest dreams—and their friends and family know it. And it's not just old friends who start taking advantage, but also people they haven't seen in years. If an athlete isn't careful, he can spend his money foolishly on a bunch of junk to impress his friends and hand out wads of cash to people who have no intention of paying him back or even being a true friend. Oftentimes, when the money is gone and the fame has faded, many of these so-called friends disappear.

But I've also seen some of these young men become wildly successful not just in sports, but also in life. Often, they had to make the hard choice of cutting off old friends and acquaintances who were dragging them down and make new friends who lifted them up. It was never easy, but it made all the difference.

Likewise, you might have to make that tough choice and surround yourself with better friends who will help you succeed, not drag you down.

Fail to Succeed

It may be easy for me to push the entrepreneurial spirit on you at this point in my life because I've seen what it can get you. However, my journey has also come with a fair amount of uncertainty and failure. Many of my businesses haven't been successful for one reason or another, but these experiences were lessons. Trust me on this: You learn way more when you're going down than when everything is going smoothly.

Nobody wants to be a failure, that's for sure, but take it from me that when it comes to failure, what you really fear are the consequences of failure, not failure itself. At the same time, there's no better education for an entrepreneur than failure. The Small Business Administration (SBA) keeps the stats on business failures and claims that more than half of new businesses will disappear within the first five years of being established.

Still, I like these odds. . . because while the failure rate may be 50 percent, the survival rate is also 50 percent! Which statistic do you see?

Rich Karlgaard, publisher of *Forbes* magazine, often says that one of the things that distinguish American culture from other cultures is our passionate belief in second acts. Even if we fail at something—or lots of things—Americans believe in the power of second chances, of starting over, learning from our mistakes and using that accumulated wisdom to succeed the next time.

I believe that one of the keys to success in life is figuring out how to master the process of failing fast and cheap, learning from those failures, and somehow fumbling toward success.

Perhaps one of the most visible comebacks in recent memory may be Mr. Donald Trump. Mr. Trump is widely regarded as having directed the largest financial turnaround in history. In the early 1990s, he was nearly $1 billion in debt. One day, Trump pointed out a homeless man to a family member and said, "See that bum? He has a billion dollars more than me." Knowing that it was going to take hard work and perseverance, Trump put his head down, learned from the mistakes that brought him to the point of near ruin, and set the gold standard for corporate turnarounds.

Today, the Trump Organization is one of the most recognized brands in the world and is diversified into multiple businesses, including luxury hotels and casinos, media, and numerous others.

There is no question that moments of self-doubt attended the turnaround of the Trump Organization. Everyone has self-doubt, and all of the biggest hurdles are internal.

> *If you're struggling to balance work and family life, you have to check out Barry Hamilton's story "Reaching for the Stars." You owe it to yourself and your family.*

Another very important point in Trump's comeback story is one of legacy. Your viewpoint on handling failure can be generational. Perhaps you grew up with parents who let failure get the better of them rather than bring out the best in them. Perhaps they stopped pursuing a dream because the going got too tough. The good news is that you don't have to live the life your family and friends live. You have the opportunity to define the way in which you'll respond to failure. You can make the difference in your family. You can be the one who changes your family's history. It's all about changing your thinking. When one person stands up for something, it might be just enough to tip the next person over and inspire him or her to also stand up.

You see, Donald Trump's father, Fred, was friends with Dr. Norman Vincent Peale. He'd read Peale's famous book, *The Power of Positive Thinking.* Trump's father's outlook on life gave Donald a huge advantage as an adult facing his own hurdles. Mr. Trump will tell you, "I'm a cautious optimist but also a firm believer in the power of being positive. I think that helped. I refused to be sucked into negative thinking on any level, even when the indications weren't great. That was a good lesson because I emerged on a very victorious level. It's a good way to go."

Types of Entrepreneurs

I hope you're beginning to understand that there's no standard formula for success. The choice is entirely in your hands, no matter what your predisposition is for personality, height, intelligence, age, life-stage, or anything else. The reality is that you have strengths, and you need to play to them. You also have weaknesses, and you need to be well aware of them. You'll have failures, and you'll need to learn from them.

To prove my point, let's take a look at three vastly different types of personalities and see how they can all lead to successful entrepreneurship.

The Risk Taker

Now we're in familiar territory. Everybody thinks of entrepreneurs as the big risk takers, right? They're the ones who jump out into the unknown hoping to land on their feet. They're always onto the new thing, constantly starting new ventures, the adult equivalent of a kid with ADD.

There certainly are entrepreneurs who are like that—but not all. You're not thinking of entrepreneurs when you stereotype them as the Risk Takers. But the stereotype exists for a reason. Those types of people generally are the ones who get all the press and hype because they're wild and exciting. When you think of entrepreneurs as being that way, you're really thinking of a type of entrepreneur. You're thinking of Richard Branson.

> **Read Dan Caulfield's story, "Carpe Diem: Seize the Day" to be inspired by a man whose passion propelled him into his business.**
>
> **Also see Jeff Benjamin's story, "The Hundred Book Rule."**

And really, Richard is the perfect example of the Risk Taker. He's a guy who oozes risk and adventure. He's well known for his transatlantic exploits, having been rescued from near death in the Atlantic Ocean six times by helicopter. He's an adrenaline junky who seems to have that Midas touch. But there's a reason Richard is successful. He has vision—and the wisdom to build a great team.

Richard is the perfect example of the fact that you don't have to be academically smart to be successful. Because he's dyslexic, he did horribly in school and even struggles with words and reading to this day. In a recent TED interview, he related a story about how, at the age of fifty, he kept mixing up net and gross income in a board meeting. After the meeting, one of his board members pulled him aside and drew him a picture of a fish in a net. "Richard," he said, "Net income is the income that is left in the net. The rest that gets away is gross income." A lot of people would let a disadvantage like that knock them out of the game. But Richard didn't let his handicap keep him back. He let his passion move him forward.

And passion is what started it all for Branson. In an interview with CBS News, Richard explained why he became an entrepreneur. It was never about money, he said. It was about passion. He started his first venture, *Student* magazine, to change the way the world thought about topics that were important to him. He started Virgin Records to create music he liked. The money was a by-product of his passion. It allowed him to do what he loved, but the money was never the motivation.

Richard has always followed his passion. Against the advice of many associates, he started Virgin Airlines. It cost him his record company. In hindsight it worked out, but could have easily gone the other way. Over time, he's learned the value of surrounding himself with a great team of advisors who complement his strengths and help keep him anchored. In fact, after Richard's last rescue from the sea by helicopter, he came home to a full-page advertisement by Virgin Airlines that said, "Richard, there are better ways of crossing the Atlantic."

For people like Richard, the challenge of entrepreneurship is finding the ability to stick with something to the end. They're always looking for the new thing, and they easily grow bored with the same old routine. Because of this, they often become serial entrepreneurs—Richard has started over 360 companies in his lifetime. The key to being a successful Risk Taker is to find fresh challenges in the familiar. To look at what you've created already and see the adventure in innovating the mundane. Risk Takers have to risk commitment—and that's harder than it sounds.

> *Make sure to read
> Amir Tehrani's story,
> "Pay Attention to the Trends,"
> for more on the importance
> of balancing action
> and analysis.*

The Analyst

Some of the most successful entrepreneurs in the world aren't risk-taking adventurers by nature. Instead, they're measured individuals who like to keep to themselves, are good with numbers, and, by carefully studying deals, can spot opportunities others miss. Think Warren Buffett. He's a perfect example of the Analyst.

If you didn't know anything about Warren, you'd have no idea he was one of the richest and most successful people in the world. He lives in an unassuming five-bedroom stucco house in Omaha, Nebraska, which he purchased in 1957 for $31,500. He drives himself to work in a Cadillac DTS, and takes an annual salary of $100,000 from his immensely successful company, Berkshire Hathaway, which produced over $100 billion in revenue in 2008. Warren leads a generally minimalistic life for a person whose net worth is around $47 billion. He's nearly the opposite of someone like Richard Branson, who jet-sets around the world and lives lavishly, yet Warren is much more successful. Warren's biggest indulgence? Playing bridge twelve hours a week.

Warren's path to becoming an entrepreneur was vastly different than Richard Branson's. Warren is an expert at analysis. The success of Berkshire Hathaway lies in Warren's ability to scour financial reports, conduct interviews, and make company tours. He spots opportunities that others miss, and he takes measured stakes in successful companies. Warren doesn't take huge risks. He's an Analyst. He takes a look at the numbers, and if they don't work out, he moves on. If they do work, he pulls the trigger.

But plenty of people are good at analysis. What makes Warren, and others like him, more successful? For one, he pulls the trigger on deals. Many Analysts don't. And at some point in their lives, successful entrepreneurs who are Analysts realize they can use their skills for themselves. They don't have to spend their life working numbers for someone else's benefit. They reach a point where they have to take a risk, step out, and make a move. And they surround themselves with people who are more risk-adverse than they are. People who recognize the value an Analyst brings to the table, who are willing to follow the plan because it's so good, and who are willing to push the envelope when the Analyst isn't.

And that's Warren's secret. He got rich using other people's money. When Warren was just starting out, he convinced eleven doctors to invest $10,000 each in his investment firm—he invested $100. Eventually, that firm grew to be Berkshire Hathaway. His $100-billion company started with $100 of his own money and a plan that attracted other people's money. People took a risk on him, and he took very little risk of his own. That's the magic of the Analyst.

The Analyst's weakness is his fear of risk. At some point, he needs to put up or shut up. There's an old term that describes the plight of the Analyst to a "T": Analysis Paralysis. Because the Analyst is so concerned with digging through every number and searching out every crevice, he or she can mentally freeze themself out of a deal and miss some great opportunities. Warren is the first to admit that he's missed some opportunities in his lifetime. Famously, he missed the opportunity to save Lehman Brothers because he didn't know how to retrieve his voice message from Barclay's Chief, Robert Diamond—though that might be more by the grace of God than a missed opportunity! To be successful, the Analyst needs to surround himself with a team that will help push him off the starting line to pull the trigger on a good deal. Analysts also have to learn to adapt and to embrace uncertainty and change, which come with the entrepreneurial territory. The world of the Sleeping Giant is an ever-shifting one.

The Visionary

A third type of entrepreneur is the Visionary. Visionaries are individuals who have an almost preternatural ability to find, master, and profit from emerging trends and markets. Many people think Visionaries are lucky. But actually, they're incredibly insightful and able to see what others can't.

A friend of mine, Tom Anderson, the co-founder of the social networking Website MySpace, is a perfect example of the Visionary. I first met Tom via an e-mail he sent me after reading my bestselling book, *The ABC's of Real Estate Investing,* which is about my current business: finding and investing in multifamily real estate in the western United States.

Tom is the classic Visionary. In 2003, he and a few computer programmers set up the first few pages of MySpace to allow people to socialize through Web profiles. As Tom says, "From the very beginning I was thinking about the social aspect—that one day everyone would have a profile, everyone would put themselves online, and that all the things you do online become much more interesting when wrapped around a profile....this was a very foreign concept in 2003—mainstream society was definitely not ready for this." In many ways, MySpace pioneered much of what we consider social media today.

The Website also revolutionized the music industry and forever changed the way bands gain fame and interact with their fans. As Sharin Foo from the Raveonettes wrote in *Time Magazine,* "For our band, MySpace is a community in which we can directly interact with our fans. It lets us skip all the layers of industry and media and speak openly and in our own voice—and get instant feedback. Before MySpace, my band partner, Sune Rose Wagner, and I knew very little about our fans. We had always followed the traditional music-business strategy of targeting a demographic and hoping that with a mass-media approach, we could reach the people. Not anymore."

When Tom Anderson and his business partner, Chris DeWolfe, started MySpace, they had a vision to create a portal Website that would democratize the Internet. And they had the vision to understand the immense potential of social media. You've surely heard of social media by now, but back then, it was just an emerging trend. Other social media sites were shutting down pages that featured bands or businesses. Anderson and DeWolfe wanted to create a forum that allowed for anybody to interact in any way they saw fit. Bands and celebrities quickly latched onto this, and the site grew to 46 million users without any advertising, just word of mouth. They were one of the first to see the potential in and leverage the power of social media. From there, the business took off, growing to over 100 million users and eventually selling for $580 million in 2005.

What you may not know is that MySpace was not Tom's first business idea—and it won't be the last. There is no question that Tom understands social media and the complexity of computer programming, a skill he learned completely on his own. His focus was never on the money, but rather on having fun and giving his customers exactly what they wanted. Money wasn't his passion—it was love for the work.

The money flowed as a result of his skill and passion—and his unique vision—not the other way around. As Tom puts it, "If you do what you love, you are likely to find more success than the guy who is trying to earn a buck. When you love doing something, it's not 'work,' and you'll put in more time than someone who's just punching the clock."

As with many Visionaries, Tom was very focused and very future-oriented. He recognized his inexperience in starting an actual business. Though he had great ideas, he knew that ideas weren't enough. He needed solid structures and great business acumen. He needed a great team.

Tom's business partner, Chris DeWolfe, was key in helping MySpace become a successful company. Yet he also found a partner who knew the importance of leveraging the ever-changing world of the Web. "The thing I like about Chris," said Tom, "is that he's not like all the other people I've met in business. He's able to cut to the chase right away. We don't waste time on things. We didn't sit down and write up this big plan and spreadsheets and try to force that imagined plan. We've been quick and nimble on our feet. I was working from common sense. Even though Chris does have that background, he's never been pushing me to that mold, and he doesn't follow it himself."

The key to being a successful Visionary is to balance pushing your vision forward and finding the right players to implement it well.

While these very different entrepreneurs all became very rich, they all have many similarities. They were never focused on the amount of money they would make. Rather, they were focused on personal and passionate missions, and from there, the money flowed. This is an important distinction. They truly love what they do, which is probably the most important point. If you're doing what you really enjoy, it never feels like you're working.

The Breaking Point

People with vastly different personalities and backgrounds can be successful entrepreneurs. No matter what your situation, you can make the choice to join the New Business Class—to join the Sleeping Giant. But you have to make a choice.

Everybody who does anything of value in this world comes to a point where he or she has to either press forward or give up and fall back on the same old patterns of fear and self-doubt. I call this the Breaking Point. When you come to your Breaking Point, you will either break through and experience a thrill like never before—or it will break you. And you'll go back to putting your hopes and dreams on the shelf while helping other people achieve theirs. Which will it be for you?

You have what it takes. But you have to make the choice.

For the Risk Taker, this means recognizing the fear of commitment and personally accepting the challenge of focusing on making innovation in the mundane. Not doing so means abandoning great opportunities and leaving behind the wreckage of half-completed projects and disappointed people. At some point, Risk Takers have to drill down and ride a wave to shore. When they choose to accept that challenge, the sky is the limit.

For The Analyst, this means pulling the trigger on that deal. It means stepping up and taking a risk, and trusting in your team and investors to help you step onto the surfboard to begin with. At some point, you have to stop waiting for the perfect wave and just take one. Otherwise, everyone will have fun without you, and before you know it, the party is over.

For the Visionary, it means looking at your skill set, teaming up with others, analyzing the trends and taking advantage of them, and realizing that there will always be the next opportunity, just like there was with MySpace.

I can't tell you what your Breaking Point is, but you know. Maybe you're approaching one now, or maybe you've come to the Breaking Point already and been broken. Whatever your situation, you have the opportunity as you read this to engage or reengage your Breaking Point and to break through. What's it going to be?

The Anatomy of an Entrepreneur

So you're ready to join the Sleeping Giant. You're ready to be an entrepreneur. You've realized the huge opportunity ahead if you will only take that bold move to go for it. You've realized you have something unique and special within that you can bring to the world, and that you're capable of leveraging your strengths and overcoming your weaknesses to find the freedom you're looking for in life. The freedom to spend more time with your family, freedom to make your own schedule, freedom to be your own boss, and freedom to pursue your passions and build something important—something the world needs, with your vision and energy.

> *If you think you can't change the world through a concept, you need to read Rommel T. Juan's story, "It's Not about the Money."*

But inspiration will only take you so far. I think we all know that. There are practical things that come along with being an entrepreneur. These are things that, coupled with your confidence, passion, and energy, are essential to being successful in business. I call them the Anatomy of an Entrepreneur. Just like a perfectly working body, you need all these parts to be whole and healthy as an entrepreneur. And you need all parts working together in harmony to really take off and do well.

Concept

You could have all the enthusiasm and ambition in the world, but if you don't have a good concept into which to pour that enthusiasm and ambition, you'll get nowhere. Every great entrepreneur has a great concept. Henry Ford wanted to build a self-propelled carriage, and he invented the automobile. Richard Branson wanted to bring great music to the world and change culture with ideas, and he started Virgin Records and *Student* magazine. Warren Buffett wanted to find great investments and pool other's resources to acquire them, and he started Berkshire Hathaway. Steve Jobs wanted to make computing personal, and he invented the Macintosh computer. Tom Anderson wanted to create a portal on the Internet that allowed for people, bands, and organizations to fully express themselves, and he started MySpace.

> *Read Derek Volpa's story,
> "Your Business Is Right
> in Front of You," and see
> why you don't need a
> big business plan to succeed
> —and for proof that
> they really do end up
> in file cabinets!*

None of these men created a company and *then* found his great concept. They had a great concept and build a great company around that concept.

Don't let this discourage you. You might think that you don't have a great concept—or any concept at all. That's not true. You just haven't articulated it yet. If you've ever solved a problem on the fly, if you've ever contributed a great plan that improved your company or department, if you've ever fixed something no one else could fix, you have within you the ability to bring a great concept to the world.

It doesn't have to be brain surgery, but it does need to be specific. If you think about it, you only need someone to believe in it and to buy your product or service. That's it. If you try to develop a concept that's not unique and highly competitive, your chances for success will be lower. If your concept is "one of a kind" and something people want, your chances of success will be higher.

For instance, when I started my last company, I wanted to find great apartment investments to provide high returns to my investors; to provide excellent, well-managed housing for hard-working Americans; and to provide jobs and fulfillment for my employees. We wanted to bring The Good Life to our investors, customers, and employees. We determined that the best way to do that was to invest in what are known as B-class apartments—apartments that are predominately geared toward blue-collar workers. That's all we invest in. Our product, B-class apartments, is a concept that works well for our investors and us. We've built our company around it, and we now employ over 200 people.

Before we move on, discover your concept. Don't let fear of failure hold you back. Think big. Chances are you've seen something that could be done better. You can build the better mousetrap. You can revolutionize that industry. You can bring meaningful change into the world and into your life by being true to your dreams and passions.

And if you have a concept and you've discounted it, you need to revisit it. Why did you put it on the shelf? Was it really a bad concept, or were you afraid it was too good? Sometimes we're more afraid of success than of failure. Either way, you need to take that concept, believe in it, and run with it.

And you need a plan.

Plan

A lot of people get hung up when talk about a business plan starts. They think business plans are for Harvard MBAs or for seasoned executives.

Jonathan Davis gives some important pointers on the topic of flexibility in business—and life—in his story, "Uncertainty Can Be Empowering."

They think of tons of market research and shudder at pulling together a monster business plan that will really impress investors.

But you want to know a secret? No one reads your monster business plan. Usually those become paperweights or get stuffed into a file cabinet to die a slow death.

That doesn't mean you can move ahead without a plan, however. But for your great concept to succeed, you must have a great plan too, especially if you're raising money from investors to fund your idea. It just doesn't have to be a book. You still need to do market research. You still need to run some models. And you still need to have enough information to convince people that your concept isn't only worth getting on board with, but also worth investing in, either with time or money.

Here's what I suggest: Pull out a single sheet of paper. Write down your concept. Then write out a concise plan for how to make that concept successful. Then do your market research and run your numbers. Revisit that plan and make adjustments as necessary—but keep it to just a page or two.

And you don't have to do a five-year plan. Unless you're a prophet, you have no idea what's going to happen in five years anyway. Do you think people who had five-year plans in 2005 were still thinking about those plans in 2010 after the worst financial crisis since the Great Depression? No. If they were smart, they were thinking about how to take advantage of the reality of today—not some imagined tomorrow. Focus on short-term goals that can move you toward success, and be ready to adjust on the fly. Your plan needs to be flexible enough to change with the times, but it also has to be solid enough to build on.

Here are some things you should include in your plan.

The Concept. Write down the concept and the reason why you're so passionate about it—why you know it will succeed and why people will want it.

The Market. Do your market research and make sure you know your customers, what they want, and how much they'll pay for it.

The Need. Determine what you need to make your concept a reality and to build your business around it.

The Execution. Put on paper short-term milestones to achieve your goals and meet your needs.

Most importantly, don't get married to your plan. It will change. Be willing to be fluid and think of your business plan as more of a guide. As Jason Fried and David Heinemeier Hansson write in their book *ReWork,* "Plans are inconsistent with improvisation. And you have to be able to improvise. You have to be able to pick up opportunities that come along. Sometimes you need to say, 'We're going in a new direction because that's what makes sense today.'"

> *Check out Blake Canedy's story, "Being Homeless Is a Good Motivator," to learn more about the importance of flexibility and being in the moment.*

Partners

As we've discussed, everyone has strengths and weaknesses. The most successful people in life, those who really achieve their goals and dreams, are those who understand the need for partners. Great partners can come alongside you and supplement your weaknesses and enhance your strengths. They can fill in your gaps and be a major part of getting your business off the ground and beyond. And you can do the same for them.

For more on the importance of partners, make sure to read the story by Adrian Li, "From Classroom to Boardroom."

My first company, McElroy Management, was a good company. We had a solid client list and great income. We provided exceptional service and had a fantastic reputation. But once I met my business partner, Ross, and merged my company with his to form MC Companies, I realized how much more I could do as an entrepreneur. Today, my company is much larger and more successful because of the skills and strengths Ross brought to the table. And the same is true for him. Finding the right partner was the most important business decision I've ever made.

And that brings up an important point: Don't rush into partnerships. Just like a marriage, a business partner can be a great thing or a devastating disaster. And while you'll never know definitively if a partner will work out, you can definitely limit the possibility that he or she won't work out by being clear about what you're looking for and your expectations.

Have high standards and don't compromise when it comes to your partners.

Money

Money is a tool. And it's an important one. For your business to be successful, for your concept to change the world, you must either find a way for it to be profitable or obtain funding to get it there.

Check out Neil Balter's story, "The Twenty-Year Ovenight Success Story" for lessons on the importance of employees and how to hire the best.

Also see Paul Lepa's story, "Big Margins Can Mean Big Business."

There's no formula for funding your endeavor. Just like anything else in the world, you have to examine your circumstances and adapt your strategy to them. For instance, Warren Buffett pulled together doctors to invest in his opportunities by offering what high-income earners with little spare time needed—an investment opportunity with high returns and minimal effort. He identified those who would benefit from his product and targeted them successfully. Richard Branson created a magazine and sold enough ad space to cover his printing costs. From there, it was a matter of selling enough magazines to keep advertisers happy and to net a profit. Tom Anderson created a space online where advertisers could target millions of people with precision like never before.

Many would-be business adventures are stalled because the entrepreneur thinks he has to somehow pull together a ton of investor money, like venture capital. And certainly some businesses require that, but many don't. The key is finding a path to profitability any way you can. Because as Jason Fried and David Heinemeier Hansson write in *ReWork,* "A business without a path to profit isn't a business, it's a hobby."

Be inspired by Richard Levychin's story, "Follow the Cash," about how he developed a successful company while working part-time.

Finding profitability might mean operating your business on the side while you work during the day, building to a point where your hobby can support you and become a business. Or it might mean having such a compelling deal that people can't pass it up and get in line to invest. Both have happened, and both are viable. It will depend on your life stage, your personality, and the type of business you're starting.

Make sure to read Carol Frank's story, "Choose Your Partners Well," for an important lesson on what can happen when you don't do your legal work properly.

Team

When you first start out on your own, you wear a lot of hats. You have to do the accounting, the marketing, the product development, the customer service, and more. Needless to say, it's not the best use of your time being a generalist. As an entrepreneur, your job is to grow your business and innovate. That's hard to do when you're spending hours taking care of administrative details and balancing books. Eventually, you get to the point at which you need a good team.

Some people start out having their spouse handle various aspects of the business that they don't want to focus on. For some, this works. But for many, it's a recipe for disaster. Personally, I like to keep my business and my marriage separate. When

Check out Troy Hazard's story, "Remind Me... Why Did We Get Into Business?" to see how good systems benefit you and your company.

I got enough velocity, I hired an employee. Then after a while, I hired more employees. Eventually, I had enough people working for me that I could focus completely on what I'm best at—growing my business, finding new deals, and finding investors. Regardless of what you love doing most and are best at, you'll need a great team to help you get to the point

where you can focus on that most of the time.

Just like with partners, you must choose your employees carefully. Hiring and training someone is expensive and time-consuming. Having to repeat the cycle continually because you're poor at choosing employees can be more maddening than actually handling everything yourself. You need to find people who you can trust and empower to run with your business.

Legal

It can be a dangerous world out there. When you're starting out on your own, you need to make sure you're covered legally. That will mean having an attorney you trust to help you form your company as a legal entity and to help you with contracts and disputes. A lawyer can also help you set up your legal status as a company so that you can enjoy the proper tax benefits, saving you a lot of money down the road.

I find that many young and new entrepreneurs are too trusting. While it's a shame that you can't be so trusting, the reality is that you should have the proper legal protection for everything you do. That means having proper contracts for engaging clients, having rock-solid operating agreements for your partnerships, obtaining proper protections for your intellectual property, and more. I know it all seems dry, but I can't stress how important it is to be legally covered.

Trust me on this. You'll sleep better at night.

Marketing

You might have the greatest concept on earth, but if you don't have a platform to sell your idea, you're not getting anywhere. In the new economy, it's easier than ever to market your product. The Internet has completely leveled the playing field. No longer do you have to hire an expensive marketing agency to create a concept and an expensive marketing campaign for your product. Now with a Website, a blog, and Facebook and Twitter accounts, you can create a real and meaningful groundswell. But it takes commitment and authenticity.

In the new economy, people know when you're selling them a bill of goods. If you're truly passionate and believe what you're offering can change the world, well then, so will others. Not only that, but more than likely you'll gain fans who will take charge of promoting your product for you—for free. It's a brave new world, and it's opening doors for tons of entrepreneurs, busting through the traditional barriers to entry. One of the most important things you can do, and what should be a main priority, is to get the word out about you, your company, and your concept.

Systems

As you gain more and more traction, you'll find that being more productive will become more and more important. The easiest way to achieve productivity and accomplish more in less time is to develop solid systems. Good systems make your team and company run more efficiently because people can be trained easier and more quickly, anyone can learn the systems and step in to handle work overflow, and there is never a question about how something should be done.

Good systems empower your people to take ownership—and they keep you from having to explain the same thing over and over again.

A Final Thought

As I mentioned, I've had the privilege of being part of Entrepreneur's Organization for more than eleven years. EO is one of those special organizations that brings together some of the best and brightest business minds in the world simply for the sake of free exchange and encouragement.

> *Matt Shoup's story*
> *"You're Fired! Now What?"*
> *is a must-read for learning*
> *how to angle your business*
> *when marketing to*
> *successfully complete a sale.*

In the process, incredible things happen. In a sense, EO is the prototype of the incorporate economy I talked about earlier in this Introduction. The organization exists solely to bring together like-minded entrepreneurs in the spirit of cooperation and to help one another become successful. It's a great organization with a great mission.

EO is a pioneering organization. Its members are people who've paved the way for the Sleeping Giant. They've laid the foundations of the New Business Class. EO members were entrepreneurs before many people knew what the term meant. Their trailblazing paved the way for entrepreneurship to enter the mainstream. Today, you can even take entrepreneurship courses at the world's leading universities. That was unheard of when many of the EO members were building their businesses. Because of this legacy, EO has much to teach on the subject of successful entrepreneurship and even life.

Visit *TheSleepingGiant.com* for more resources, including The Sleeping Giant blog.

And make sure to sign up for your FREE monthly Sleeping Giant Newsletter, where you'll find more stories and insights on entrepreneurship.

For many years now, I've been passionate about entrepreneurship and the potential it has to revolutionize not only the lives of individuals, but also our country and the world, and I've wanted to find a way to share the wealth of knowledge collectively shared in EO with up-and-coming entrepreneurs. This book is the end result of that passion.

Here you'll find incredible stories of successes and failures from twenty of the most successful entrepreneurs in EO—men and women who took the chance. These stories contain lessons of immeasurable value. I'm a firm believer in the power of stories to not only change you, but also teach you. Reading about the practical examples and steps and missteps of these successful entrepreneurs will give you priceless insights for your own entrepreneurial journey.

These are also diverse stories. The beauty of entrepreneurship—of building your own thing—is that it's your own thing! Everybody's approach to business and path to success is different. You'll find that diversity reflected in these stories. You'll see different ways of looking at life, business, and success. Some people in the stories might even seem contradictory. The writing styles are different, and the formats vary. Each story is a perfect reflection of the author's personality and approach to life. I wouldn't have it any other way.

At the end of the day, there's no "right" way to entrepreneurship success. There's only your way. These stories provide many levels of inspiration that are sure to connect with you, whoever you are. Enjoy.

But most of all, these stories are the stories of pioneers. As I have said, it wasn't that long ago that no one talked about entrepreneurship. Most people simply wanted to find a good job after college. But times have changed. Those "good" jobs are few and far between, and the prospect of uncertain futures in corporate America has sparked a huge wave of people who believe there's a better way—that paving their own paths is the best way to fulfillment and security. The men and women you'll read about in this book are part of an adventurous generation that helped to bring entrepreneurship to the mainstream, and they want nothing more than to see people just like you become even more successful than they are.

So they're sharing their stories.

Enjoy. Read. Be inspired.

I know I was.

The Giant awakes.

It's Not about the Money

1

Binalot Foods
Rommel T. Juan

This is a true story of social entrepreneurism born out of fond childhood memories. It's proof positive that doing well in life often means doing good things for others. Rommel and his brother, Raffy, formed their company to preserve the culture of their land and to enlighten a whole new generation about traditional community and togetherness. Their mission is to be the biggest and the best. But that's just the beginning. They realized through the challenges they faced as a company that they had the power to create positive change that benefitted everyone. The question was, would they take up the charge or let it pass them by? I think you know the answer. Here's their powerful story.

—Ken

When I was growing up, business was the last thing on my mind. I had an active imagination and most of my time was spent creating art projects, reading comic books, or watching cartoons. It was my older brother, Raffy, who had the entrepreneurial flair.

His friends called him The Beijing Businessman because he always had something to sell. He peddled hard: from menthol candies to bus passengers who passed by our house when we were kids to mixed drinks to partygoers in college. Around Christmastime in 1992, during one of the military coups in Cory Aquino's time as

President of the Philippines, Raffy created "I survived the coup d'état" T-shirts. They were an instant hit. We even got bulk orders from other provinces.

I enjoyed all the training, but I found more value in the personal interactions than in the actual profit. I was proud to satisfy customers with the goods I sold. It wasn't until college that the entrepreneurial bug bit me, and it was only after being involved in a few family business ventures that I decided I wanted to do something on my own. Being in a family company was too restrictive. Every decision I made had to pass through the elders, so everything took time to develop, and my ideas weren't always welcomed.

The Birth of Binalot

Binalot Foods sprung from my favorite childhood memories. My family owned a little farm in Cavite, south of Manila, where we would go to get away from the urban hustle and bustle. My mom, Mommy Charito, would always pack our food in banana leaves, which is the traditional Filipino way for rice farmers to bring their food to work. No matter what we ate, food always seemed to taste wonderful wrapped this way, and it always made me happy.

The Philippines' colorful and vibrant traditions are a product of many influences. Three hundred years of Spanish colonization inspired our food and fiesta culture. The most popular form of public transportation is the Jeepney, an adapted military jeep left behind by the Americans after World War II. And in the Philippines, we have some of the biggest malls in Asia, which have created a strong mall culture for our youth that is similar to the one in America.

But we're also a culture of tradition. One of my main objectives with Binalot was to forge a company that is both socially responsible and culturally sensitive. It was against this backdrop that my brother, Raffy, and I formed Binalot (which literally means "wrapped"). We wanted to recreate and reintroduce a lost piece of our culture to modern urban dwellers. I also wanted to make Binalot the number-one fast-food chain in the Philippines by promoting Filipino humor, values, and culture.

I injected humor into our menu by creating corny, rhyming names for the foods such as Bistek Walastik (bistek is a beef dish marinated in lemon), and by designing the company's logo and mascot, Mang Bina (Mr. Bina), who wears a traditional Filipino farmer's costume. Our stores have murals depicting typical Filipino scenes like families eating together and people riding Jeepneys, paying respect to elders, and taking part in the Bayanihan tradition, in which neighbors all help to carry a hut home when a family wants to move.

Raffy and I initially positioned Binalot as a delivery food service and invested heavily in equipment and manpower to serve this purpose. Delivery is very popular in the Philippines because of the heavy traffic in the central business districts. It's impractical to go out to lunch since most workers only get one hour for their lunch breaks. People either eat at their workplace cafeterias or pack their lunches. Seeing customer service as our main tool for success, Raffy and I hired an army of riders and motorcycles to answer the demands of the huge customer base we were expecting.

> **Binalot Foods sprung from my favorite childhood memories.**

The company slowly gained ground, and when the delivery business boomed in the late 1990s, we hired more delivery boys, which ultimately proved to be a bad financial decision. Our peak delivery time was a small window during lunch. After that, the delivery boys had nothing to do. As a result, even when our sales were high, our labor costs ate up all of our profits, and at the end of the day, we lost money.

When we finally figured this out, we cut our delivery staff, while the ones we retained learned to multi-task. They were taught to cook and run the cash registers. Some businesses need specialized roles, but in our case, it made sense for the employees to do multiple things, both from an economic and efficiency standpoint. This seemed to stabilize us, but then, disaster struck.

The Crash of 1997

The Asian Financial Crisis gripped much of Asia beginning in July 1997. The crisis started in Thailand with the financial collapse of the Thai currency, but it soon spread throughout most of Southeast Asia, including the Philippines, where economic growth dropped to virtually zero in 1998.

This problem became my problem because by then, we'd hired a lot of riders and bought a fleet of motorcycles with a loan from my dad, and we hadn't paid off the loan. With the collapse of the economy, food delivery was way down, and it got to the point where, in one outlet alone, we had an idle staff of eighteen.

I admit there were times when we were on the brink of giving up. We simply didn't have enough experience to know how to react. I didn't even know how to analyze an income statement. My idea of business operations had always been simple: If we needed something, we bought it. Fortunately, we had the sense to evaluate and adjust our goals. We trimmed our workforce to the essential personnel and opened a store in Mandaluyong where other riders and motorcycles could be assigned. It was a smart move, but not quite enough. Delivery increased when the new branch opened, but waned and then plateaued after a couple of months.

That's when we received an invitation from a major mall food court to open a store. It was Binalot's last straw, so we decided to give it one more shot, putting all our resources into this new branch in Shangri-La Mall's food court. We set up the outlet with only 24,000 pesos ($500US). The gamble paid off. Binalot's Shangri-La branch opened to lines of people—so many, in fact, that we were unprepared. The success the company experienced with the new outlet helped us overcome our fear of shifting to another business model—the food court.

We still retained our motorcycles, but delivery was no longer our main focus. The dine-in model provided steadier sales, and the Shangri-La experience paved the way for other food court outlets to open. Having fixed-location outlets helped Binalot grow, and the company regained lost ground by the end of the year. We used each year's profits to open a new store the next year.

New Life after the Crash

From that point, it was smooth sailing. We opened new outlets at malls like Robinson's Galleria, SM Makati, MRT Ayala, and Glorietta. We also began franchising, an idea we'd considered for some time.

Initially, we offered franchises only to family and friends while we worked out the kinks of the system. But with or without kinks, franchising was a big boost to Binalot's revenue. Real growth started, with the outlets doubling from six to twelve.

Franchising and our growing confidence were a potent combination that made Binalot the number-one fast-food restaurant in the Philippines. I was also fortunate to have a strong wife, Christine, who was instrumental in my success. Before I met her I had no direction. She helped me find balance in life and a new focus.

While the company was booming, I enrolled in the Master of Entrepreneurship course at the Asian Institute of Management where, for the first time, I formally learned about business. Those lessons helped me make better use of the company's resources and strengths, and to overcome our weaknesses and threats.

For the first time, I was able to see the whole forest, not just the trees. One of our main projects was to come up with a five-year plan. This helped me study all the aspects of the business and plan for it. We also did an external environmental study and an internal assessment of our company's strengths and weaknesses. More than anything, my studies gave me an understanding of our operations. I identified my own weaknesses and hired the right people to help me maximize Binalot's operations.

That was when Binalot really grew—I was no longer holding it back. We're now growing at an unprecedented rate, and as the business evolves, our systems grow stronger.

My Humble Advice

As I said at the outset, Binalot has a vision of what it wants to be that is reflected in everything we do. The challenge now is to increase our market share and achieve top-of-mind awareness with the general public while staying true to that vision.

This is an important lesson for businesses. To have a vision, you first must define it clearly so that your employees have direction and purpose. Who wants to work for a company that operates like a headless chicken?

At Binalot, our vision is to be the largest truly Filipino fast-food restaurant chain in the country. And we want to promote Filipino humor, culture, and values. It's very clear that we want to build our brand and increase our outlets, but this approach also allows our employees to adopt a little entrepreneurial spirit of their own—to take risks and be creative.

Once you have a vision, it's also important to adapt to the changing landscape and needs of your market. We do this by talking to our customers, inviting them once a month to have breakfast with the president of the company, frontline order-takers, and cooks for a feedback session. We ask them what the customers want, why they want it, and how much they are willing to pay for it. I also visit the competitors' outlets. I look at what they're selling, what seems to be the fad, and, if the ideas are good, I incorporate them.

This is how we keep the vision and the business moving forward.

Entrepreneurship Is about More than Business

I don't know many true entrepreneurs who start their companies for money. There is always something else that encourages them to start their businesses and persist through the challenges. As our business progressed, I realized there was another, equally important purpose behind Binalot. What is uniquely Filipino (or "Pinoy," the slang for Filipino) is our hospitality, our sense of community, and our belief that we're responsible for one another.

Our fast-food restaurants celebrate everything good about the Philippines, from the traditional foods and customs to the core values of honesty, respect, hard work, and service to others.

But simply honoring our culture wasn't enough. Our company wanted to do more for our country and its people. It was that social conscience that led us to form the Binalot Foundation, a program to help farmers find diverse uses for the banana, such as making flavored banana chips or finding a bigger market for the puso ng saging, a vegetarian delight.

In many of our rural areas, the banana is the primary source of revenue, which creates a cycle of poverty. A whole day's work spent harvesting bananas and banana leaves barely earns workers enough to afford the necessities of life. We felt we could help.

It all started when my aunt brought me along to the Asian Forum for Corporate Social Responsibility (CSR), held in Jakarta in 2006. That's when I realized that CSR can become an integral part of a business, and I started pondering how we could make it work at Binalot. When the great typhoon "Milenyo" struck in 2006, its winds nearly destroyed our entire supply of banana leaves—our main packaging material. We were forced to import leaves from the Visayas provinces, which made our costs spike. That's when I decided I wouldn't let external factors affect our business. We decided to go straight to the farmers.

We found a strong source of leaves in Nagcarlan Laguna, south of Manila, and struck up a friendship with the most unlikely of businessmen. His name was Rodney Oriel, and when we met him, he wasn't even wearing a shirt. But once we told him about our plan to organize the community and provide a stable source of income, he became a crucial volunteer and liaison. The result was the Binalot DAHON community. DAHON is an acronym for Dangal at Hanapbuhay para sa

Nayon, which means "Livelihood and Dignity for the Rural Community."

We trained the community about how to supply us with raw banana leaves, but we also taught them to add value by cutting the leaves, trimming them to our specs, and cleaning them. We'd been paying Manila rates for these services previously. Now through DAHON, we were able to give elderly women who had previously had no source of income the opportunity to make 200 pesos a day. As time passed, the women became more skilled and could finish the job in ninety minutes, and their rate of pay rose significantly. We also trained members of the community to make banana chips, which we sold in our Binalot outlets, giving them another source of revenue.

Binalot buys all the harvests from these communities, ensuring their market and income, and in turn, we have a tremendous supply chain partner. There is no question that the program has been a financial win for all sides, but it has also been very rewarding on a personal level.

In fact, helping whole communities improve their standard of living has been one of the best and most unexpected side effects of my business. I'd encourage all entrepreneurs to become more involved with their communities—to find ways to help the less fortunate and to incorporate these ideas into the fabric of their business plans. We plan to replicate the DAHON program in other areas where Binalot hopes to expand.

Final Thoughts

Our community programs make business about more than just money. I'm passionate about this side of what we do, and I encourage you to determine what you're passionate about and pursue it. I know that sounds obvious, but passion is essential if you plan to stick with anything as you grow older. Let me tell you a story from my own country.

Big Chinese business tycoons in the Philippines and around Asia are called Taipans. There are well-known Taipans in the Philippines such as Henry Sy, Sr., a Chinese Filipino businessman and founder of SM Group and chairman of SM Prime Holdings, the largest retailer and shopping mall operator in the Philippines; John L. Gokongwei, Jr., a Chinese Filipino businessman with holdings in telecom, financial services, petrochemicals, power, aviation, and hog farming; and Lucio Tan, who owns Asia Brewery, Tanduay Holdings, Fortune Tobacco, Philippine Airlines, and hundreds of other companies.

All have vast business empires, and all these men are past seventy years old. But they're still actively working. I heard our Senator Manny Villar (himself an entrepreneur) speak once, and he said, "The reason these Taipans don't retire is because they enjoy every minute of what they do. How can you ask a painter to stop painting? How can you ask a singer to stop singing? How can you ask an entrepreneur to stop creating business?"

There is a great potential to make it big as an entrepreneur in the Philippines. In fact, the Philippines needs more entrepreneurs to help the country's economy, unemployment levels, and to give people a more positive outlook on life.

Entrepreneurs are, by nature, positive thinkers. They dream of a better life and then they make it happen. Find a way to make your dreams and the dreams of the community around you come true, and success will be yours.

Rommel Juan is Co-Founder and President of Binalot Fiesta Foods, Inc., a major franchise with forty-two food outlets in metropolitan Manila. Binalot proudly serves its clientele their favorite Filipino food the traditional way—wrapped in banana leaves. Under its Corporate Social Responsibility Program, the company has helped the farming community by getting banana leaves direct from the farmers to eliminate the middlemen, and teaching the village women to cut and pack the leaves, which provides jobs. Rommel has been featured in multiple magazines and newspapers including *Entrepreneur Magazine* and *The Manila Times,* and has made appearances on ABC and CNN. He is a sought-after entrepreneur, speaker, and advisor.

Big Margins Can Mean Big Business

2

PearlsOnly
Paul Lepa

This is an amazing story about a guy who had no plans on becoming an entrepreneur at all. He simply bought a necklace for his mother at a market stand in China, shipped it home, and the rest is history. But in between that somewhat ordinary event and his amazing success, Paul Lepa stumbled upon a little-known technique that every entrepreneur can use to his or her advantage. I won't tell you what it is, but as you read his story, it will become clear to you. In his recounting of the early years, you'll learn concrete business lessons, but you'll also discover that you can change paths and do something you've never done before. Believe it or not, you can become an expert at something much faster than you think. Embarking on a whole new career adventure is not only possible, but potentially profitable too.

— Ken

Imagine that your company is selling $3 million a year in the United States, Canada, the United Kingdom, and Australia, with a customer base rapidly approaching the 100,000 mark. Picture each employee, equipped with Standard Operating Procedures, Policies, Human Resources manuals, and reports. Turnover is low. Simply put, things are stable. You devote a scant ten hours a week to daily operations, and the goods and services that you need become cheaper and cheaper because of the volume of business you're doing. Team leaders run their various sections. There's a calm and peace in the business. You're not afraid. You're confident. And as such, you're aiming to grow to $125 million in sales over the next five years.

Now imagine that none of this is a dream, and that it all started four years ago in a bustling market in China. That's my story.

I arrived in Beijing, China in 2003, working for a big multinational corporation. The company paid for my apartment, gave me a car allowance, and paid me a tax-free six-figure salary. I had six weeks of holidays, some of them fully paid. It was a comfortable and easy life, but it was somehow unsatisfying. There was no challenge, no fulfillment, and the monotonous climb up the corporate ladder was becoming repetitive and downright boring.

One day, I found myself in a Beijing market, taking in the local wares. The market sat amid the urban sprawl of the city, and countless wooden tables were piled high with anything that might sell, from fresh fruit to knock-off tennis shoes. The market was loud with voices haggling over prices in Chinese and English. The smell of fish and motor scooter exhaust was heavy in the air. There, I bought a strand of pearls for my mother and sent them home to Canada. She had them appraised, and I got a call from her shortly thereafter, chewing me out for spending $500 on pearls instead of saving my money. Little did she know one remarkable fact: I'd only paid $40!

I thought that maybe someone had made a mistake. I quickly sent five more strands of pearls home to be appraised. They all appraised for about ten times what I'd paid for them. I was blown away. And I realized that it was time to translate this discovery into something bigger.

Armed with this tiny piece of information and a $200 camera, I went back to the market and bought ten more strands of pearls, an initial investment of about $600. It was easy: I used PayPal to get money from Canada and my little camera to snap photos of my product.

I needed to describe the products, and I didn't know much about pearls. So, I also ordered five books so I could read up on them. I asked people in the Beijing market about pearls, taking in information on what they were all about. Unconsciously, I'd begun to *educate* myself on the product. Not only was this easy, but it also was fun, interesting, and exciting.

I launched a little Website called PearlsOnly.com. Google had just gone public, and their AdWords program was the latest rage. I took advantage of the program and began advertising on Google.

Initially, I kept prices low, charging only twice what I'd paid for the pearls. Imagine the feeling when the first order came in! The adrenaline mounted, and so did the sense that I was onto something big. Between June and December, I continued to grow the site. The pearls continued to sell, and my costs were substantially less than what I sold the goods for. I made $45,000 in sales in my first five months.

I've always loved technology, but I was no e-commerce expert. So, again, I had to learn. I'd read somewhere that reading ten books on a given topic would give you more knowledge on the subject than 80 percent of the people out there. So, each time I needed to educate myself to face a new challenge, I simply bought ten books on the subject and consumed them. I devoured new information like I was starving for it. I worked, and I read constantly. I started putting long hours into reading, because there seemed to be so many new things on the horizon that I needed to prepare for. There were a myriad of questions to which I didn't know the answers. How and why did people shop on the Internet, and what would make them happy? The questions kept coming up, and so I just kept reading.

> *...I realized that it was time to translate this discovery into something bigger.*

I probably read well over 100 books and e-books in my first year of business, as well as countless articles. The hours continued to pile up. I was still working at my corporate job, but when that workday ended, I'd work on developing *my* job, the one I was carving out day by day. In addition to my forty hours per week for the corporation, I was spending an additional sixty to eighty hours on my business. Weekends evaporated. That time was now devoted to study. I'd become a monk holed up studying the ways of pearl distribution and Internet commerce, and before I knew it, that feeling of rising to a new challenge was back in my life.

My diligence paid off, and the site sold more and more. I learned that site design was important, so I found a designer to work on PearlsOnly Version 1.0. What I'd read was certainly true—my sales doubled overnight. I read more about Google and AdWords, got smarter, and again, my sales doubled. I forecast that my sales for the first full year of operations would generate around $225,000 in total sales and

$100,000 in profit.

But there was a catch. I was getting *very* tired. I was pulling double duty by working two jobs, and my corporate work was becoming an impediment to my Website work. However, I was still getting more money from my corporate job than I was from my budding pearl business. I was scared to leave my stable job and the cushy lifestyle that the company offered and plunge into the risk and the unknowns of the pearl business.

But I loved the Website work, and I'd grown to love the pearls. What I didn't love was my corporate job. It was time to commit to one or the other. The fear was crippling. What if sales dried up or people stopped buying? In the end, it was my wife who encouraged me to discard that fear. If it didn't work out, jobs were plentiful. So, despite my fear, I gave up the ease and safety of my 9-to-5 job, taking a dive from my rung on the corporate ladder, and committed fully to PearlsOnly on October 10, 2004.

With that change, the pressure immediately increased. I was struck by the knowledge that the sole income for my family was coming from this business. I'd expected my hours to decrease, but they increased even more. But the revenue kept climbing, too. Everything began to come together, piece by piece, like a puzzle.

Employees came on board. At first, they were students with no experience in packing and shipping. I was personally handling site maintenance, customer care, design, and shipping issues. My employees had no experience, and their "help" tended to cause additional headaches and further drain my time. I was working up to 120 hours a week, but even though all of this was exhausting, it was exhilarating. My future was in my hands alone.

By 2004, we had eight employees and were making $1.2 million in sales. I was the pillar on which the business stood. All the questions came to me, and all the decisions were mine to make. Any balance my life had had before had been shattered. On a normal day, I might handle customer support, resolve a shipping problem, or even fix a total site crash. I was making about the same amount of money as I had at my previous job, but I was working three times as much. Doubt started to seep in through the cracks. I didn't have time for friends or family. I'd been consumed by my success.

I began to realize that my overworking was just another problem that I had to solve. Since I didn't know how, I fell back on what had worked for me all along: The Ten Book Rule. This time, ten books didn't do it. It took thirty or forty to educate myself on how to actually run a business of my own, and as the fog of doubt cleared, the answer became visible: *I couldn't do it all myself.* I needed to hire smart people who would work for me without draining my time.

The process wasn't easy. I set up organizational charts, mapping out various functions of the company. I knew exactly what I needed, but it would take six people to fill the man-hours I'd put in. It wasn't so much that I was some sort of Superman. On the contrary, I was a generalist. I needed to bring specialists on board to get the job done right.

So, I started hiring. An IT manager was my first great hire, and his expertise decreased my workload dramatically. I could breathe again. He also taught me one of the most valuable lessons I would learn: Documentation was a necessity. Before, I'd despised the mechanical and technical processes, the procedures, and the documents. They all felt so "corporate." But I came to understand that documenting ideas was the only way to transfer this information from my head to those working for me. If I wrote it down clearly, I could simply give it to new employees to learn. It was a perfectly simple concept, but to me it was a "Eureka!" moment.

I applied my Ten Book Rule again to learn about documentation—how people did it and what it meant. Slowly, step by painstaking step, I managed to extract myself from the everyday grind of the business. I was no longer *in* the business, but was now truly *running* the business. It hadn't been easy. My health and relationships had suffered, but the business had grown.

Looking back at five years of growth, I would do some things differently, and some I would do the same way.

Things I would do the same:
1. The Ten Book Rule: I loved it then, and I love it now. I plan on sticking with this for the rest of my life.

2. Vision: I had a vision of how I wanted my business to perform and an idea of what it should look like long before that picture materialized.

3. Organizational Charts: Having a map of the company layout, even when my name was in all of the boxes, showed me where

I needed to hire.

4. Self-funding: Investors and venture capitalists are a complication
   I had no interest in dealing with.

Things I would do differently:
1. Hire early: I should have taken the hit to my wallet and hired high-
   quality experts early on, reducing my workload in the beginning.

2. Documentation: I'd begin documenting and writing down how we
   were doing things early on—staff transitions during start-up
   are frequent, and this would've helped with the learning curve.

3. Scalability: I'd control the rate of growth, slowing it down to better
   manage a balance between my work and my personal life.

PearlsOnly.com has been a dream born out of the most unlikely of circumstances. Today, with every pearl we select and every strand we ship, we know
we're bettering the lives of people around the world. Are pearls my passion? They
are now. That and knowing that an idea that started so small could grow so big and
make something as beautiful and perfect as pearls affordable to more people. I hear
it from our customers all the time: Our work matters.

PearlsOnly.com

A marketer at heart, Paul Lepa managed to overcome the
challenges of linear thinking from his electrical engineering
background to blend technology, sales, and marketing into
one. Paul is the CEO and Co-Founder of PearlsOnly.com, an
e-commerce company with nearly 100,000 customers in the
U.S. and the UK and over $10 million in sales to date. Before
founding PearlsOnly.com, Paul held a number of different positions, including Senior Account Executive at Telvant in Calgary, Canada, and Director of Global
Pipeline Solution Unit at ABB in Manheim, Germany. After relocating to China,
Paul decided to take the leap to start PearlsOnly.com.

Reaching for the Stars

3 Red Canyon Engineering and Software
Barry Hamilton

Some people know what they want to be right from the get-go. They're born with it, and they go after it with everything in them. Others abandon their dreams when plan A doesn't work out, and they go on to live a life of compromise. That's not Barry's story. Here's a guy who took his dream and ran with it. And decades later, he's still as charged about his passion—space exploration—as he was when he was a kid. But today, there's more to his incredible drive and his high risk/high reward endeavors. There's a new passion, one that would spur him on even if everything else was gone. And it's a passion our world desperately needs.

—Ken

What did you want to be when you were five years old? A fireman? A veterinarian? A rock star? The President?

I wanted to be an astronaut. I still do.

I was only two years old when Neil Armstrong and Buzz Aldrin first stepped onto the moon. I remember watching the subsequent missions up through Apollo 17 in 1972, when I was five years old. Those images of men on the moon stayed in my psyche and never let go.

My mom was mesmerized by the same images, and we huddled together around the television each time a rocket went up. She was an electrical engineer at Hewlett-Packard, and she appreciated the kind of technology that this mission required. But, like millions of other Americans, she also sensed there was a great historical significance to this event. It touched her on a deeply emotional level. Her reaction had a profound impact on me, and when I look back on it, I think that's why I wanted to become an astronaut. I mention that because I've always believed that you have to have a passion for what you do. A lot of people say that, but what does it really mean?

To me, it means you have to love what you do with every fiber of your being. It has to be as important to your heart and soul as it is to your head. If it isn't, it won't work because you'll never get through the severe emotional, physical, and financial valleys that will come, no matter how well you plan or how smart you are. I didn't know the meaning of the word "entrepreneur" when I was five, and I certainly never entertained the possibility of being one when I enrolled at the Air Force Academy in 1986. I just wanted to explore space. Later, I found out my eyesight wasn't good enough to make it on board a NASA spacecraft. I had to move to Plan B. You might say I modified my dream, but I wasn't about to abandon it.

Ramen Noodles and Restless Nights

What I remember most from my first year of business is how cheaply I lived, how hard I worked, and how little I slept. I'm sure a lot of entrepreneurs have similar stories. I'd been out of college for nine years, but during that first year of business, it felt like I was back in my old dorm room, pulling all-nighters so that I could cram for a big exam. The problem was that there was an exam every day, and my livelihood depended on passing every one.

I'd just joined forces with two other engineers—one of whom is still with me—to form this cool company with a great name: Red Canyon. Red Canyon is an aerospace company dedicated to making a big difference in space. Our capabilities extend into electrical, software, systems, and mechanical engineering; research and development; and space operations. Our clients include NASA, the U.S. Air Force, Lockheed Martin, Northrop Grumman, Ball Aerospace, and Raytheon. We've been involved with several major missions—from searching for water on Mars, to analyzing the composition of distant comets, to building the next human spacecraft (Orion) to service the space station and fly to the moon and Mars.

Despite how exciting that may sound, there was nothing glamorous about Red Canyon's first year. That year, I ate mostly Ramen noodles and bean burritos and worked around the clock. If I remember right, the burritos were made from canned, refried beans because you could get three cans for a dollar. That kind of lifestyle sounds crazy when you think of the large-scale work we were doing—developing flight software for satellites that explored Mars, the sun, and comets for Lockheed Martin.

Even though we got our work done on time and on budget, there was a ninety-day gap between when we paid our employees and when Lockheed paid us. It made growing the business difficult, and pinching pennies became a way of life. Our work seemed exciting, cutting edge, and important on the outside, but actually, it was just like any other business with realities like accounts receivable and payroll. Nothing shot you back down to Earth faster than processing payroll tax forms.

Since we had to pay our employees first, my partner and I didn't even take paychecks. I got creative when it came to saving money. I lived on credit cards and at one time put over $200,000 on credit cards just to make ends meet. Not knowing when I was going to be paid next was incredibly stressful. And

> *To me, it means you have to love what you do with every fiber of your being.*
>
> *It has to be as important to your heart and soul as it is to your head.*

it was exhausting trying to predict down to the penny employee payroll and other expenses just to keep the business going.

The second year of the company wasn't any less stressful. Since I knew we needed more than one customer, I interviewed for and landed a flight software position with Ball Aerospace on what turned out to be one of my favorite projects, Deep Impact—a NASA space probe designed to hit a comet, make a crater, and study the impact and interior composition of the comet as it spewed into space.

Back then, I worked thirty hours a week for Ball on Deep Impact, and I still put in forty hours at Lockheed while I finished testing flight software for the Genesis spacecraft. After having been in space for several years, Genesis captured solar particles and dropped them into the Utah desert. I commuted from central Denver to Boulder and then to south Denver every day.

This three-hour round-trip commute, combined with the hours at Lockheed and Ball, created fifteen-hour work days, six days a week.

Lessons Learned

You learn a lot of lessons your first years in business, and looking back, I made it harder on myself because I didn't delegate. I even did my own bookkeeping. I'd lay out all my bills on the floor in my office in a carefully developed system for determining which bills could be paid last and which had to be paid right away. Then I'd make partial payments, knowing that my creditors would keep working with me as long as I stayed in contact. I knew the game, and unfortunately, it was one I had to play.

Here's another hard lesson—inefficient use of resources. Many people told me to hire someone else to do the bookkeeping, but I couldn't. I needed to be in control. It was like solving a 1,000,000-piece puzzle every month, and I got really good at it. But it was a poor use of my time.

There were huge drawbacks to my control obsession. The worst part was the toll it took on my relationships. My fiancé and I broke up, and I split with my business partner in the third year of business. There was no question that the business was adversely affecting many aspects of my life. It was an awful time for me personally, and it definitely affected my mood and my spirits.

I know it sounds like I should have quit the whole thing many times over, but in spite of all my challenges, I still had this firm belief that Red Canyon was going to make it. It was where I was supposed to be; it was who I was. That belief helped get me through the tough times. Besides, I wasn't employable anymore. What would I do? I have always had an independent streak, and I found out early on at the Air Force Academy that I was really lousy at taking orders. So even if everything had gone downhill at Red Canyon, I knew I'd just have to start another company. But I didn't like the idea of starting over again, and I was determined to make Red Canyon work.

Staying Power

They say it's always darkest just before the dawn. Red Canyon's darkest days turned into endless laborious nights—until daybreak finally came in the form of a satellite designed to study the climate on Mars. Landing the Mars Reconnaissance Orbiter (MRO) mission work was a huge win for us.

It was our largest contract to date: a $3-million project to develop flight software and operate the spacecraft. Our team wrote the memory manager software, which helped prolong the mission in 2009. We also developed the telecom software, which enables the satellite to communicate with Earth. Today, we still have engineers sending commands to the spacecraft and monitoring its status so NASA can continue to gather climate data about Mars. Getting this job was a big feather in our cap. It gave us a lot of street cred in the industry, and I know it was a direct result of the success that we'd had on the previous Mars programs with Lockheed.

Because of MRO, I was able to not only graduate from eating bean burritos to eating salads and fruit, but I also started paying down a significant portion of my debt. It wasn't long before I got to a point where I could finally pay myself every week.

That's when I took a breath (and exhaled, too). It was the first time I actually looked back at what had just happened. When you're in the early stages of a new business, and you're just trying to survive, there's not a lot of time for big-picture perspective. Sure, you're doing daily analysis to discover what works and what doesn't work, but there's no time to gather your thoughts and experiences to strategize for the next phase.

Through all of this, the big "aha" moment for me was that you must have the right people on board with you. Writer Jim Collins said it best in his book, *Good to Great:* You have to get the right people on the bus. Having the right people on the bus means you can get more work done, but I discovered an added benefit. If you have the right people and you're driving in the wrong direction, someone on the bus might save you by saying, "Hey, we need to turn left here." And that can save you a lot of heartache.

In my case, I didn't have that person on board in the beginning. I gave over half of my company to a partner whom I barely knew. I nearly lost the business and our customers due to our disagreements over where the company was going. The best advice I can give anyone starting out on his or her own is to surround yourself with smart people whom you trust. If I'd had a few trusted advisors in my corner, I would've never made the decision to bring on a partner I hardly knew.

People Person

I learned my lesson, and these days I surround myself with friends who always come through for me. I know a lot of people say, "Never go into business with your friends," but for some reason, that strategy has worked out for me. A lot of my friends have become my co-workers, partners, or employees, and a lot of my co-workers have become my friends. I think it's just the way I operate. I've been in the industry for nineteen years, and I've learned to rely on my network. I'm a connector.

When you have confidence in your people, they'll help you succeed. Today, I know I can rely on my friends, and that ability has also paid dividends through Entrepreneurs' Organization, a group of like-minded entrepreneurs. More than anything, EO has taught me to focus more on my family. So many of the members have gone through similar experiences and similar personal hardships. They've helped me understand the mistakes I made with my family.

Now that I've assembled a great team, I have a lot more time to spend with my family. I'm about to be married, and there's nothing more important to me than being a good partner and a good dad to my two kids. The financial gains of my business haven't hurt, either. It gives you the freedom to make life easier for your loved ones. I'm working on wills and trusts—things I never gave much thought to before. I won't repeat the same mistakes of the past. I'm starting a life with someone, and I'm ready and excited to embrace that responsibility.

The Next Chapter

I may not wear a space suit or swing golf clubs on the moon, but I'm an entrepreneur doing my part to help all of us reach the stars. I also believe I'm inspiring the next generation to continue that journey. Somewhere, there is a little kid surfing the Internet right now who is imagining what's out there, just like I did with my eyes glued to our TV screen so many years ago.

Maybe that kid is even dreaming of becoming the first person to walk on Mars. I remember the feeling all too well. I do what I do because I still have that feeling. I still want to discover what's out there and to be a part of space. But today, I also do it for the next generation of space explorers, scientists, and engineers. If there were nothing else in it for me, that alone would be enough.

Red Canyon
Engineering and Software

Barry Hamilton is founder and CEO of Red Canyon Software, an aerospace technology company focusing on satellite flight and ground software. He is also CEO of BareRose Real Estate, which owns and develops over $20 million of both commercial and residential real estate in Colorado. Barry serves on the advisory board for the Leadership Program of the Rockies, is the small donor committee chair for Colorado Aerospace, and volunteers at the When I Grow Up Foundation, WB2 Mile High Skies College in Colorado, and Monticello Club.

Pay Attention to the Trends

4

Conrad Asher Licensing Group
Amir Tehrani

As I talked about in the Introduction, many good ideas are squelched and many opportunities are missed by analysis paralysis. This is the rare story of a highly analytical entrepreneur who did all the research, and then did more research—and still more research—and actually pulled the trigger. It's a testament to the fact that research absolutely pays off. In fact, it helped Amir avoid a lot of rookie mistakes. He had a passion for starting a business, and he was going to find one....he just wasn't going to fail at one.

—Ken

Question: What do a bakery, a tequila company, and a real-estate developer have in common? Answer: They were the inspiration for my entrepreneurial pursuits. Confused? Let me explain.

I was raised in an entrepreneurial family. My parents, all my aunts and uncles, and my grandfather were entrepreneurs. So naturally I grew up with an entrepreneurial mindset. My family always encouraged me to get my feet wet, get experience, and ultimately, to do something on my own. It was good advice, and I listened.

After my undergraduate work in economics and computer science, I wound up working for Deloitte Consulting. It was an amazing training ground and a great place to "get my feet wet," as my family of entrepreneurs would've said. The high caliber of people who surrounded me, and the number of different companies and industries I saw in a very short span of time, all contributed to my early real-world learning. I couldn't have asked for a better first-job experience.

The typical systems analyst project lasted four to six months. I spent time working with companies such as DirecTV, Washington Mutual, Hewlett-Packard, and AT&T. In every instance, I interacted with senior-level management, consulting with them on basic strategic-management techniques while learning the inner workings and philosophies of those very successful companies.

When I went back to business school, I decided that once I'd finished my advanced degree, I'd never work for anyone as an employee again. I worked very long hours at Deloitte and was frustrated because I didn't see the direct benefit of my hard work. I knew I wanted to be an entrepreneur and felt that business school was the perfect launching pad. Figuring out what my entrepreneurial pursuit would be became my two-year mission at UCLA.

Initially, I started looking at the Baby Boomer generation, an unbelievable demographic 50 to 60 million strong with an incredible amount of spending power. I looked into everything from pharmaceuticals to dental cosmetics to hair coloring—anything I could think of that might appeal to a Baby Boomer as he or she aged. After all, there were lots of Baby Boomers, and that fact alone could make for a great market.

But for one reason or another, nothing seemed to click. Either I just couldn't get excited about a product like hair dye, or, in the case of biotech, there was too much competition and the barriers-to-entry were too high.

Between my first and second year at UCLA, many of my classmates were going off to internships at various big-name companies, but I also had a number of friends who were starting their own companies. I was with three of them as they opened the doors to their offices, and I noticed they all had one thing in common: They were catering to the Hispanic market. One was a Mexican bakery, which has done quite well; one was a tequila company; and one was a real-estate development company focused on the Hispanic demographic.

That's when the light bulb went on in my head, and I realized, "Wow, all this time I've been looking at Baby Boomers when the real trend is the Hispanic demographic."

Survey Says

From my perspective, the Hispanic demographic is highly underserved. You don't find consumer options available for them as you would find for other demographics. Big companies have done some research on the segment, but nothing deep or meaningful. Companies are literally forcing Hispanic consumers who aren't getting the products they want at the big stores to shop at the local tiendas (shops). There, Hispanic consumers are getting some of their wants fulfilled, but not all. Tiendas are small and can't carry a wide variety of merchandise. There are no tiendas that come close to the selection of a mass retailer like Target.

I find this an amazing fact when you consider that the Hispanic demographic is extremely young and has an incredible amount of disposable income. Their spending power is surpassing a trillion dollars and will double in the next five years. Potential is everywhere.

Buying power was just one of several advantages of the Hispanic market that I discovered during my research. Another was Hispanic media. They'd figured out how to target the market very effectively. As with merchandise, there is a limited supply of media available to the Hispanic consumer, so the market has few choices. That provides a tremendous opportunity for the existing media and for other businesses trying to reach the market. In essence, it's a captive, unfragmented audience.

Another significant advantage of the Hispanic demographic is the nature of its geographic distribution in the United States. Eighty percent of the 40 million Hispanics in the U.S. are concentrated in five states: California, Texas, Illinois, Arizona, and Florida. That's very cost-effective from a business standpoint. If you focus your resources on those five states, you don't have to worry about the others states and you can still be successful.

These research findings planted the seed in my head that the Hispanic market was my calling. I knew I wanted a business with hard inventory that I could touch, feel, and control. I didn't want a service-based business, and I knew I was not a big knowledge guy who could create software or a dot.com company and come out on top. That whiz-bang approach was not up my alley. I needed an old-economy type of business—one that I could have created twenty or thirty years ago.

One of the best decisions I ever made, and one I'd recommend to others, was to settle into a niche business. If I were ever to start another business, I'd stay in a niche market. You can command a premium in terms of your margins, and you can fully target your audience through advertising, whether it's cognac drinkers or clothes horses. You can be an industry leader.

With all this information as a launching pad, I started traveling to Mexico and staying with friends there. Eventually, a friend introduced me to a man working for the Mexican Soccer Federation (Federacion Mexicana De Futbol). As I looked into it more and more, the passion this country and the Hispanic demographic had for soccer—a passion that really hadn't been tapped in the U.S.—got me more and more excited. I could see and feel the energy, but, being an MBA, I had to conduct a survey before I was fully convinced.

From my perspective, the Hispanic demographic is highly underserved.

You don't find consumer options available for them as you would find for other demographics.

Big companies have done some research on the segment, but nothing deep or meaningful.

The premise was simple: If I could better understand this market, I would have powerful insights into consumer behavior. Of the 40 million Hispanics in the U.S., 30 million are Mexican, so it made sense to focus on the Mexican market. I surveyed 500 Mexican consumers in Los Angeles and asked them one question: What are you passionate about? There were only three general answers, and they validated my initial thoughts. The first answer was church. The second was family. The third was soccer—and they weren't always in that order.

Futbol Frenzy

Soccer is the only sport Mexicans follow in their country, and the only one that has pro leagues. They're very passionate about soccer in Mexico, and they remain passionate about it when they come to the United States.

When I stumbled upon the Federacion Mexicana De Futbol, I realized that they had very poor merchandising practices in the United States. Counterfeit goods were rampant. The quality was shoddy, and there were issues with marketing and distribution.

This was it! This was the opportunity I'd been looking for. I partnered with the gentleman who facilitated my introduction to the Federacion, and I set out to acquire the exclusive distribution rights to market their apparel in the United States. I made full use of my MBA negotiating skills to strike a deal.

Then, with a Mexican business partner, we also negotiated deals with the top teams in Europe like Manchester United and FC Barcelona. As with the Federacion teams, we retained the exclusive distribution rights to these European teams. It was a logical leap. Many of the best Hispanic players go to Europe because of the high quality of the European leagues and the high pay scale. By landing those clubs, we became a one-stop shop for Hispanic consumers. Now it was time for distribution.

Targeting the Big Box

The Hispanic market garners a lot of attention from retailers like Target and Walmart. You'll find Hispanic foods like refried beans, tortillas, and jalapenos there, and they carry Mexican brands that are household names for Hispanic customers just as Heinz is for American customers. These retailers are always looking for products to offer to the Hispanic market. In fact, they have teams of people dedicated to that very task. As you can imagine, when we came to them with our idea, we offered a solution to their problem with apparel.

The first retailer we approached was Target. We were in within six months, which is unbelievable when you consider the difficulty other vendors experience getting in those doors. Some people wait ten years to get a meeting with Target. Our product initially rolled out to fifty stores.

Once we were in, we didn't face many setbacks. In fact, our sales were off the charts. We were outselling Adidas four to one in those stores, and the Target folks were obviously happy. They'd never seen anything like it.

The next thing we knew, we were on a plane to Target's headquarters in Minneapolis. They asked us one thing: How quickly can you expand? Naturally, we got right on it, but we had some small hiccups along the way. We had some difficulty navigating their online vending system, which caused some laughs on both ends, but there was never anything big enough to doom us.

Today, we're in our fourth year as a business. In the first year, we grew about 400 percent, last year we were up exactly 200 percent, and this year we're up almost 200 percent. The growth is a testament to the rock-solid research we conducted prior to launching our business.

I think the reason we've been able to grow so much during the worst recession of our lifetime is the fact that the Hispanic market, while not unaffected, is less affected by the sour economy.

By and large, the Hispanic market does not own real estate, so the housing crash hasn't impacted them like it has people in other demographics. They can't get credit cards, so the credit crunch hasn't really affected them either. They don't own stocks, so the stock market crash was of no concern. About the only thing that's hurt them is that construction and services are down. Consequently, unemployment has hurt their communities, but not as much as it has the greater American market.

From Me to You

As I consider the past four years, a few points jump out that warrant sharing. First, I was very fortunate to partner with the right person. There's a certain art to finding the right business partner, and there's also a certain amount of luck. I've always liked collaborating with people, but I've had some bad partnerships along the way. I've learned you can't rush the process and that being thoughtful and patient pays off when it comes to selecting and taking on a partner.

Second, I'm thankful every day that I chose a niche market. It allows me to focus my energies in a narrow corridor and really master what I do.

Third, I did my research and examined my market. I gained valuable insights that helped me better position my products and anticipate demand.

The premise was simple: If I could better understand this market, I would have powerful insights into consumer behavior.

Here's what I mean: Most people assume the Hispanic market is one big, likeminded demographic. We figured out in our first year of business that the Hispanic market breaks into two segments. One is the Mexican who just arrived in the U.S. in the past five years. He doesn't speak English well, or at all. He may not even have proper papers or documentation. He's a day laborer who's sending money back home. He's extremely conservative, extremely religious, and very responsible, which is why a family that pooled all of its resources in search of a better life sent him to the U.S. in the first place.

The other segment is the Mexican-American. He's a second- or third-generation American and likes to wear baggy clothes and get tattoos. He follows the Raiders, the Dodgers, and USC football. He grew up in urban, inner-city areas like L.A., and he thinks of himself as more American than Mexican.

Knowing the difference between these two segments helped us design two entirely different apparel lines, one for the conservative immigrant, and one for the urban Mexican-American raised on rap culture. The lesson: Do your homework and know your market.

All that being said, the most important thing is to just go for it. My research was valuable, but I may have overanalyzed the opportunity in an effort to answer every question. It was my way of doing the work and perhaps delaying the decision to pull the trigger. It took me six months!

In the end, I couldn't anticipate everything. Eventually even I, with all my research, had to just take the leap. I was lucky that everything worked out, but I was also lucky the opportunity was still there when we finally decided to move. I could have lost that opportunity by overanalyzing.

Whether your business is Mexican pastries, tequila, real estate, or soccer apparel, trust your intuitive nudge. Get as much information as you can, but don't delay. Your great idea might make someone a millionaire. Wouldn't you'd rather it be you?

 Amir Tehrani spent several years in management consulting for Deloitte Consulting and working with senior executives in Fortune 100 companies in a variety of industries. He then funded and became president of a company that acquired the exclusive U.S. distribution rights to several top Hispanic brands, including the Federation of Mexican Futbol. Amir currently holds board positions with Tabletops Unlimited, Allied Imex, Conrad Asher Group, and cPrime Inc.

A Twenty-Year Overnight Success Story

5

California Closets
Neil Balter

I've known Neil for a long time, and he's a no bull kind of guy. You won't get a lot of fluff in this story, and that's why I like it. Neil had a good idea. He worked hard doing the work that most people would never do, and through it he built a company that made its way into the stratosphere of business. That was a long time ago, and the value of this story doesn't come from his being in the moment; it comes from his wise perspective. If only we could look down at our businesses once in a while, rather than be in our businesses, we'd make much better decisions. Thankfully, we can learn from Neil's example.

— Ken

I wish I could thrill you with the lessons I learned in my first year of business. The truth is, my first year was defined by tough, blue-collar labor—and by reckless youth. I was seventeen years old when I started California Closets. I had hair half way down my back, and was partying like crazy. The first time I made $500 in a day, I felt like I'd won the lottery.

My journey began after I'd just graduated from high school and decided not to go to college. My brother, on the other hand, was in a chiropractic college. Needless to say, my parents were horrified by my choice. I was raised in a Jewish family, and not going to college was about the worst sin I could commit. When my mom asked me what I wanted to do, I told her, "I want to be a carpenter."

"Son," she said, "There really aren't any Jewish carpenters in this world." Then she paused for a moment. I'm sure it was for dramatic effect. "There was one a long time ago who had much better connections than you have," she continued, "and look what happened to him."

While it's true that I started California Closets as a carpenter, I didn't remain one for long. I found out that I had to become a businessman to take my company to new heights.

The fundamental reason why California Closets became successful is simple: It was a good idea. People have been organizing closets since the Stone Age. The difference was that nobody had ever made it into a business before me.

> *My journey began after I'd just graduated from high school and decided not to go to college.*

But the value of my story doesn't come from my first year of business. It comes from the wisdom I've since gained—what I call the 20,000-foot view. And that's what I'd like to share with you here. I'll be candid about my mistakes, and I'll call out the pitfalls with the hope that you won't fall into them too.

Where do entrepreneurs make their mistakes? Why is the failure rate of new businesses so high? What are the common denominators? Here's my take.

Mistake #1: Not counting the cost

People talk the talk, but they don't walk the walk. They say, "I'll do whatever it takes to be successful," and they do—for the first few months. They start their business all revved up. They think they're going to be the head honchos behind the desk, pushing all the buttons and smoking the big cigar. But if it were easy to be an entrepreneur, everybody would do it. It's not easy. And very few do it. It requires long hours, hard work, and usually lousy pay at the beginning.

Here's how I spent my first high-powered year in business: rummaging through people's houses and installing particleboard in their closets. Of course, only after I'd constructed the shelves outside in a carport with plastic hanging down the sides to protect the materials from the weather. Pretty glamorous, huh?

So let me ask you: Are you prepared to work your tail off and make little to no money for a whole year? It's a pretty safe bet that's how it will be. Most people get tired of working six and seven days a week with little in return. Eventually, they give up. And that's one reason why businesses fail. You'll find as I did that starting a new business takes a huge, long-term commitment. It requires planning, and realistic expectations don't hurt either—particularly early on. Still on board?

Okay. Time for mistake number two.

Mistake #2: Not having enough capital

New businesses are almost always undercapitalized. As a result, it takes longer to make things happen. Not only do you make less money than you thought you would initially (see Mistake #1), you also don't have the money to invest in building your business. The reason is that you don't acquire enough money to begin with.

I discovered that when it comes to raising money, you always need to raise more than you think you need. If you think you need $100, get $150. If you think you need $200,000, get $300,000. You never get in trouble by being overcapitalized. I'm not even sure that's a word, but you get my point. Remember that cash is king.

Mistake #3: Hiring poorly

Be careful who you hire. If you have a best friend you've know for thirty years and you want to get rid of him, give him a job. He'll hate you in six months. Hiring friends and family doesn't work. I know that's not an absolute, but it holds true in my experience and in the businesses I've watched.

In 1985, my business was growing big-time, so I hired a CEO to help run it. I believe to this day that, at some point, he decided he was going to try to take over the business. He got us into a huge amount of debt, some of which I think was manufactured. We couldn't pay our bills, and then like some kind of white knight, he rode in and offered to buy the business to save it.

I was within a week or two of losing California Closets. Fortunately, I had a mentor who wrote me a check and bailed me out. I fired the CEO, and we got the business turned around. But I learned an important lesson: People will take advantage of you. I was twenty-five, had a new Mercedes and a house on top of the hill, and I thought I knew it all. I was also young and immature, and I was willing to go along with everything my CEO said. That was a dangerous combination, especially when predators are out there.

I'm a pretty optimistic person, but I hate partnerships. I don't think they work out. In my experience, I saw many of our franchises start out as partnerships, but very few made it. The problem revolves around two core issues: Either there's not enough money to go around, or there's too much money to go around. Either way, you've got conflict. Someone has to be the boss.

The things that I generally tell people not to do are the things I did myself. I made pretty much every mistake you can make at some point in my business. And that leads me to mistake number four. I see a lot of other people make this one.

Mistake #4: Getting cocky

When you're young and you have enormous success early on, you get this feeling of invincibility. Your ego gets really big because people keep putting you up on a pedestal and you believe all the hype. I didn't get that really big knock on the head until after I sold California Closets, but that experience with my first CEO was certainly a wake-up call. Everybody can fail.

Now that I've told you what *not* to do, let me suggest a few things you should do.

Should-Do #1: Hire people who are better than you

Strong-willed entrepreneurs have a tendency to want to make every decision. They don't like bringing in smarter people. It bruises their ego. You're supposed to be the smartest guy in the room, right? The one with all the brilliant ideas, right? It doesn't work that way. Nobody is good at everything. I'm certainly not. And you're not either. There's always someone smarter than you. The person who makes every decision in the business can never grow the business. If you try to control everything, you train your employees to defer to you—and you train them to fear risk.

At some point, after you've hired the right people, you have to let them do their jobs. You can't be looking over their shoulder every minute, second-guessing their work. Criticism crushes enthusiasm. If your people stub their toes every so often, so what? Let them learn from it and move on.

On the flip side, if you make a bad hire, and you will, cut the cord quickly. You'll find yourself falling into the same trap most entrepreneurs fall into when they hire someone who isn't working out after a couple months—you just keep hoping the employee will come around. Here's the bottom line: If you've truly given the employee the tools needed to succeed, and the person is still not any good at the end of the second month, the employee isn't going to be any good at the end of the third month or the fourth, either. And the deeper and longer you go, the more it costs you and your company.

The same applies for business in times of economic hardship. I saw this current recession coming a few months before it arrived. When it did arrive, I laid off a bunch of people. Then I got everyone else together and said, "Listen, we just had to lay a bunch of people off, but we're not laying anyone else off. Don't worry whether you'll still have a job six months from now. You will. So, just do your job." If you have constant turnover in your business, people will always worry about security rather than doing their work. When you need to make cuts, make them deep so that you only have to make them once.

Should-Do #2: It's what and who you know

When California Closets started growing by leaps and bounds, and we were franchising all over the world, we could have gone into kitchens and bathrooms, too. But every time I try to expand into something other than core strengths, I might as well just give my money away. It never works out. I know how to make money in the closet business because I've experienced the business from the ground up. If I get outside of it, who am I? I'm just another guy in the vending machine business or the flooring business.

I think you can be more successful when you're known for something. I still have outside forces pulling at us to try other ventures, but closets are our niche. So we stick to what we know, rather than trying to be all things to all people. Find a niche, fill it, learn it inside and out, and do it better than everybody else.

Should-Do #3: Seek out mentors

As you fill your niche, you'll experience some roadblocks. I was fortunate that in every instance where I needed guidance to take California Closets to the next level, I found it. Without my mentors, I'd never have been successful.

My best friend's dad financed my start-up costs, and then he helped me get the word out with small-scale advertising. Another mentor took me to the next level by getting me to clean up my look and encouraging me to franchise and advertise my business. And my last mentor, Bill Levine, taught me how to manage my finances. Don't be afraid to ask for help. If you don't ask, you won't receive—that other Jewish carpenter said that. If you do ask, it just might help you succeed beyond your wildest dreams.

When I started California Closets, I was an original. Today, the closet business is part of our culture. My $2,000 investment has turned into a billion-dollar industry, and I've sold franchises in New Zealand, Japan, Australia, Canada, and many other places. The failure rate for new businesses may be high, but so is the reward if and when you succeed. In fact, building a business from the ground up is one of the most fulfilling achievements you'll ever experience.

As I wrote in my book, *The Closet Entrepreneur:* If I can do it, so can you!

Neil Balter was seventeen years old when he started the California Closet Company, an idea that came to him after his parents kicked him out of the house. He combined his carpentry skills and entrepreneurial spirit, and worked out of a van. He grossed almost $60,000 his first year and sold the company to Williams-Sonoma, Inc. before he turned thirty. Neil is a founding member of the Young Entrepreneurs' Organization and a speaker on a variety of topics, including "What It Takes to be a Millionaire Before 30." He was recognized in *Entrepreneur Magazine* with an Outstanding Entrepreneur Achievement Award and featured in *The Wall Street Journal, Forbes, People,* and on "The Oprah Winfrey Show," as well as in 500 other newspapers, magazines, and TV shows.

Choose
Your Partners Well

6   Avian Adventures
Carol Frank

Carol Frank may be passionate about pets, but she's just as passionate about making sure entrepreneurs don't make the same business mistakes that she did. Carol's honesty in admitting her shortcomings and revealing her failures is rare and valuable to any business owner. Will this story prevent you from making the same mistakes? Remember about crossing your "Ts"! Carol proves that the best lessons are learned from experience and worth every amount of sweat, strife, and sorrow.

—Ken

As a former CPA with a master's degree in business administration, I've always considered myself business savvy. My natural demeanor is to look for the best in people, trust them when they give me their word, and try not to rock the boat by being too hard-nosed. That was the foundation for starting my third company, Avian Adventures, which designed, manufactured, and distributed birdcages for high-end pet stores. Since most people have never met someone who manufactures birdcages, you can imagine that one of the first questions people ask when they find out I own a birdcage company is, "How did you, a former CPA, get into making birdcages?"

The answer becomes clearer when you discover that I'm passionate about business, networking, animals, and the intersection of the three. Avian Adventures was my third company in the pet industry, and these weren't your grandmother's birdcages. They were designer-painted stainless steel cages that retailed for between $300 and $2,700, and they were promoted as upscale furniture for you and your feathered friends.

My motto in doing business is that if you can't be better or different than your competitor, you're wasting your time. So I called a close friend, Joel Hamilton, who had a master's degree in landscape architecture and years of experience as Supervisor of Birds at the Dallas Zoo, for help.

"I want something unique," I told Joel. "Something that won't be confused with my competitors' cages—a cage on which we will be proud to put the name Avian Adventures."

Joel put pen to paper and in no time came up with several signature designs. Meanwhile, I went to work finding someone who could manufacture the signature Avian Adventure cages, and I found that someone in Monterrey, Mexico. His name was Sergio—a furniture and satellite dish manufacturer. He was eager to partner with me on this venture, and I was enthusiastic to work with him as well.

Meanwhile, I'd already laid the groundwork for distribution here in the U.S. A serial networker and natural leader, I was the first vice president of the Pet Industry Distributors Association (PIDA), and I leveraged that position to establish a network of contacts with the largest pet supply distributors in the United States. I was in business!

The response to my designer birdcage was phenomenal. By August 1996, Avian Adventures had orders in-house for over 1,000 cages, with no end in sight. Retailers wanted them, and my manufacturer, Sergio, easily kept up with demand. It was a relief to me that Sergio and I were developing a solid, friendly relationship. I even found time to attend his twenty-fifth wedding anniversary celebration in Monterrey.

Business grew, and so did the need for a signed contract with Sergio; believe it or not I still hadn't crossed that "T." In a way, our friendship made it all the more awkward. I tried negotiating a contract several times, but Sergio had acquired additional partners to provide capital to grow his business, and they wanted to play hardball with this American gringa.

They came back with some extremely unreasonable requests of my company, such as no warranty period, no responsibility to replace defective parts, and the right to reproduce the cage anywhere they wanted without consequence.

At this point, with new orders coming in weekly, I did what I'd rarely done in life—I took the path of least resistance. Business was going well, and I figured international contracts were difficult to enforce in Mexico, so I didn't press the issue. Based on my established relationship with Sergio and the exuberance of my success thus far, I placed my business' future on those two imposters named hope and assumption.

In June 1997, I invited Sergio to be my guest at the pet industry's largest trade show. Although things were going well, there were some minor complaints from retailers about details of the cages and the packaging. I thought it'd be best that Sergio hear about these

> *My motto in doing business is that if you can't be better or different than your competitor, you're wasting your time.*

concerns from the shop owners themselves. I thought it would impress upon him the need to fix the problems.

During the trade show, I pointed out the booth of a much-larger competitor. I explained to Sergio that the company had asked me earlier that year if they could buy Avian Adventure cages for resale. Since I was barely keeping up with the demands of existing customers, I declined, and I was even more adamant about it when I later heard from reliable sources that the company was going to outsource their own manufacturing to Mexico in an attempt to put me out of business.

I went on to tell Sergio how important it was to keep up the quantity and quality of our product since we were going to have this new competitor vying for our cage business.

Sometime during that fateful weekend, Sergio walked into the competitor's booth and introduced himself to the owner with a smile and a cold-blooded handshake. "I make cages for Avian Adventures, and I would like to make them for you," he said. Jesus was betrayed with a kiss; I didn't even get that courtesy.

A Bird in the Hand and a Knife in the Back

This clandestine backstabbing began to unfold over the next several months. By July 1997, Avian Adventures was on track to do $2.5 million in sales for the year. Customers were waiting upwards of eight weeks for their shipments because of the backlog created by the success of the product. Then, in the middle of a particularly crazy and seemingly prosperous summer morning, Sergio called and said, "Carol, we will no longer ship you any product unless you pay us up front."

"What!" I exclaimed. "Are you kidding? We have over $100,000 in orders ready to ship! I've been paying you within fifteen days. What are you going to do with my cages if I can't come up with the money?"

I got my answer.

Lesson #1:
Don't do business without a contract, no matter how many wedding-anniversary parties you've attended.

My first mistake was ordering even one cage without an exclusivity agreement.

My second mistake was not getting a patent for my birdcage design.

Things only got worse. In October 1997, one of my best customers, Mike, called. He said, "Carol, I just got a call from one of your largest competitors. They offered to sell me Avian Adventure cages."

"No way!" I replied. "They must have offered you cages *similar* to our cages." No one could be that stupid, underhanded, or ballsy, I thought to myself.

"I'm afraid not," Mike answered. "They told me that they had made a deal with your manufacturer in Mexico to buy your cages."

Each word felt like a slap in the face punctuated by a punch to the gut. I'd transformed Sergio, a small-time satellite-dish maker, into a multimillion-dollar birdcage manufacturer. And this was his idea of saying gracias. But my anger at Sergio's betrayal was tempered by the anger I felt toward myself. My intellectual capital had been stolen, and I could've prevented it!

My competitor repeatedly contacted almost all of Avian Adventures' customers, trying to steal my business. I was saved only because I'd forged solid relationships with my customers. I lost only one out of ten customers directly to my competitor.

During the four years I bought cages from Sergio, I knew I needed a second manufacturing source for my product. "Sourcing, sourcing, and more sourcing," was a mantra my Entrepreneurs' Organization's forum members would urge repeatedly. But it was just so easy to keep buying from one person who really knew what he was doing.

My first mistake was ordering even one cage without an exclusivity agreement.

My second mistake was not getting a patent for my birdcage design.

A "Customs" Solution

In August 1999, while still buying from Sergio, I researched having my cages made in China. It was then that I discovered that U.S. Customs detains shipments that infringe upon copyrights, trademarks, and patents at the border. For example, if U.S. Customs discovers a container full of jeans with a Levi's logo on them, they contact Levi Strauss to ensure that the jeans are legitimate. If they aren't, customs agents will seize the shipment. My original copyright lawyer never told me about this program.

Remember having options? That goes for legal counsel as well. If a doctor told you that you had a terminal condition (which in effect this situation was for Avian Adventures), you'd get a second opinion. Having only one lawyer means having only one perspective. In all fields, and especially in a field as malleable as civil law, a second and third opinion can mean the difference between life and death for your business.

I immediately registered my copyright with the U.S. Customs Department and flew to their Laredo office to meet with an inspector. I put my hope for justice into the hands of the federal government. It came in the form of a phone call I received from Sergio in early November of 1999.

"Carol!" Sergio screamed. "What do you think you are doing, holding up my shipment at the border?" Oh, sweet, sweet revenge. I could hardly control my excitement. I'd been waiting for this moment for two years.

"You're going to ruin my business!" he went on to say. "I'm not going to ship you another cage until you release the shipment that's being held by Customs." At that moment, I didn't care whether I ever sold another birdcage again; I wasn't going to give in to this man, and I was already finding new options.

"No," I replied. "I won't release that shipment just because you're threatening me. I don't care if you make birdcages for someone else—just don't make them look like mine."

Sergio backed down. "I have a new design that doesn't look like yours, and I can e-mail you a picture of it tonight. If you approve, then perhaps you can release the shipment back to me in Monterrey, and I will rework the cage with the new design," he said.

For the first time in over two years, I felt hopeful that the nightmare of having my cages sold by a competitor was coming to an end. Looking at the pictures of the new design, I was ecstatic to see that the cage was sufficiently different from mine that people would no longer confuse our cages. I would no longer have to endure the pain of people approaching my booth at trade shows with puzzled looks, saying, "I thought Avian Adventures went out of business."

Some days are better than others. This was one of those days. In an ordinary life that wasn't destined to test the limits of passion and persistence, my story might end here.

In the fall of 1999, the Mexican Trade Commissioner referred me to yet another potential manufacturer, Alejandro. I received a beautiful sample from him, and that, combined with the fact that his brother-in-law lived in Dallas, gave me enough confidence to not only place an order in December 1999, but to also do something I'd never done before—send an advance to Mexico for over $11,000. I was sure I finally had a viable backup to Sergio. But the perils of not having a proven backup manufacturer were about to hit home.

La Cage aux Folles: The Lawsuit

Convinced that I'd won a major battle against Sergio in the "war of the birdcages," I forged ahead with my best design ever, which, of course, I patented immediately. Unfortunately, on January 13, 2000, one month after sending Alejandro his first order, a process server from the Dallas County Sheriff's Office walked into my office and served Avian Adventures, Inc., and me personally, with a lawsuit naming us as defendants.

My competitor was suing me for fraud, deceptive and unfair trade practices, and unfair competition.

Furiously flipping the pages of the thick document, I found Exhibit A, an affidavit signed in October 1999 by Sergio, three days after his shipment was detained at the border. The affidavit, which is as legally binding as if the signer were under oath in court, stated that Sergio was making birdcages before I met him in 1995, and that he was the sole author and original designer of the birdcages named in my copyright.

Later, Sergio claimed, in a subsequent phone call, that he didn't know what he was signing (even though he has an MBA from Tulane and speaks fluent English), and that he was fully aware that he wasn't the original designer of the Avian Adventures cage, only that he had made some improvements in the way it went together.

After four years and millions of dollars in business, I stopped buying from him that day. I placed a call to Alejandro and asked him if he was ready to take over all of my business. Of course, he eagerly said yes, and I pulled all of my business from Sergio and gave it to Alejandro. Fortunately, I still had nearly every bit of correspondence I'd ever had with Sergio, not to mention Joel's original drawings with dates and signatures. I wasn't worried about losing the suit; I was worried about how I was going to pay for it.

Lesson #2:
Keep all supplier and customer documents and communications, and be familiar with your insurance policy coverage. When in doubt, ask.

The fourth lawyer I consulted on the matter told me to submit this lawsuit to my insurance company under my business liability policy. Sure enough, they reluctantly came back with an agreement to handle the suit "with reservation." That gave them the option of going to court to have a judge determine whether we were entitled to coverage, and subsequently the insurance company filed a lawsuit against Avian asking the court to determine who had responsibility for paying for the suit. It took more than two years, but we prevailed—thankfully, because the suit ultimately cost over $250,000 in legal fees.

In the meantime, I tried to keep Avian Adventures alive. During February and March 2000, I sent Alejandro orders for 800 cages totaling over $150,000. During one of my many visits to his factory, he looked me straight in the eye and said, "Carol, don't worry. I guarantee there will be no problem having 1,000 cages made by the end of March." Orders were pouring in.

The first ship date came . . . and went, with assurances from Alejandro that the next date would be no problem.

The second ship date came . . . and also went. After the third missed ship date, I began to worry that I'd made an enormous mistake. It was April 19th, and my customers were wondering where their product was. I'd promoted this new product full force, and they were getting impatient waiting for it.

The lesson here: Always under-promise and over-deliver.

Not having product for two months would wreak havoc on anyone's cash flow. To make matters worse, I'd fallen for Alejandro's sob story that he had to have $70,000 to start production since my order quantity had increased so much. Normally, I'd never have sent money to a manufacturer until I had finished product, but I felt backed into a corner because I'd already cut off Sergio.

I asked Alejandro repeatedly to send back some of my money. "I am going to get a bank loan and send you back some of your money shortly," he constantly insisted. No such bank loan ever materialized, and I later discov-

> *Each word felt like a slap in the face punctuated by a punch to the gut.*

ered that Alejandro's modus operandi was to ask for advances on new projects so that he could pay off old debts.

Lesson #3:
There's no such thing as too much due diligence, and when you put all of your eggs into one basket, it can turn you into a basket case!

Sales plummeted 85 percent in that one year! There were many days when I wanted to crawl back into my beautiful birdcage and quit! On one side, I was facing bankruptcy and the possibility of being someone's employee for the first time in almost twenty years. On the other side, I had a great product, a loyal customer base, and most importantly—*passion*. I just couldn't give up on my dream of making my livelihood by helping better the lives of companion parrots.

Not only that, but even with all the problems we had, the demand for our cages never let up! Our customers were loyal, understanding, and generous. One even loaned me $200,000 to keep me from filing for bankruptcy!

It Ain't Over Till the Birdcage Lady Sings

The lawsuit, which clearly started out as a ploy by my competitor to "squash us like a bug," turned in our favor. I'll spare you the gory details, but I countersued and years later, we settled the case. I came away with enough money to pay off all the short-term debt incurred keeping my business alive and have enough working capital to resuscitate an ailing Avian Adventures!

Our lifeline extended from the U.S. to Asia, not Mexico, this time. Sales steadily quadrupled over the next five years, and in August 2007, I sold Avian Adventures to one of the largest supplier of dog cages and accessories in the U.S., Midwest Homes for Pets. The sale allowed me to realize my dream of moving to Boulder and focusing on a speaking and consulting career.

Above all else, in every aspect of my life, I seek the freedom of having options. I simply will not be tied down to one offer, one consultant, one expert, one lawyer, one manufacturer, one realtor, or one anything. Why? Because more than the financial success, more than the legacy building, and more than passing fancies like acclaim and prestige, I value my freedom. That's why I went into business in the first place.

And even when I lost, I didn't lose the lessons.

Carol Frank is a principal of BirdsEye Consulting, helping pet companies launch new products and better utilize their resources. She is CEO of WholeLifePets.com, an e-commerce site specializing in natural pet products, and a managing director of SDR Ventures, an investment-banking firm. Carol is author of the highly acclaimed book, *Do As I Say, Not As I Did! Gaining Wisdom in Business through the Mistakes of Highly Successful People.* She's made appearances on "The Oprah Winfrey Show," MSNBC, "Good Morning, Texas," and NBC News and has been featured in *The Wall Street Journal, The New York Times, Entrepreneur,* and *USA Today.*

Follow the Cash

7

KBL
Richard Levychin

Richard is in this book because he looked inside himself to reignite his passion for his craft and his career. Too often, would-be entrepreneurs leave jobs and start businesses just like the ones they left with the hopes that working for themselves will bring the excitement back into their work life. They think that the potential of making a lot of money will fulfill them. There's nothing wrong with wanting to make money, but the entrepreneurs who can bring something deeper, something more primal into business are the most successful. Richard has a unique heritage and, as you read this chapter, you'll discover how that one aspect of his life has become the foundation for his enthusiasm and his success.

—Ken

I'm what you'd call an accidental entrepreneur. My business just showed up. It was April 15th, 1986. I'd just finished my tenth busy season in public accounting, and I was exhausted. Going through my latest job search, I'd interviewed with a CPA firm that felt my skill sets were a perfect fit for them. They offered me a position, working either full-time or part-time, my choice. It was spring, and I was 27 years old, had no wife, no kids, no car, and no mortgage or debt of any type. I lived in a large one-bedroom apartment in Park Slope, Brooklyn, and I split the $550-a-month rent with my girlfriend. I decided to work three days a week with the firm.

The official story is that I built my own firm on the four days I wasn't working that other job. The truth is that it was summertime—so, I played hoops. I went to the beach, I shopped, I worked out, and I got back in shape. I was making pretty good money working 12-to-14 hours a day for those three days at the firm, and my expenses were low. In 1986, the Mets won the World Series, and in January 1987, the Giants won the Super Bowl. I was living with the love of my life, who would become my wife two years later, and I was having the time of my life.

In my mind, I was always planning to get a real job and "grow up" at some point—just not then. My plan was to figure it all out in October, but when October came around, I decided to take some more time. I'd been working in accounting firms since I was a sophomore in college. By the time I was a senior, I was doing audits, which was ridiculously advanced stuff for a kid. All that experience helped me get a lot of offers when I graduated. I worked for a Big Four firm for four years, then a mid-sized firm for a while.

I always expected to be one of those guys who slaved away until retirement. Then, one day, I woke up exhausted from the long hours. I was tired of it all. The fulfillment I found in my career had waned. I realized I needed to take some time for me. So I did. And I liked it.

But a funny thing happened. While I was out enjoying my four days off each week, I started picking up clients. I wasn't looking for them. I'd just run into someone or meet someone through a friend, and they'd ask me what I did. Next thing you know, I'd have some work. Maybe it was because my head was so clear and my mind was so fresh. Maybe I was projecting confidence because I looked good and I felt good. Whatever the reason, people started hiring me. So, I reversed my work schedule. I started working just two days a week at the other firm and three to four days a week for my own clients.

What I've come to realize much later in life is that my becoming an entrepreneur wasn't by accident. My "accidental" journey to entrepreneurship that I embarked on in 1986 was actually the culmination of many events that had started even before my parents were born. It was a combination of my diverse heritage, my entrepreneurial roots, and the influence of a wonderful CPA whom I worked for while in college named Alan Kahn. Alan took great interest in my progress and pushed me beyond what I thought were my limits. My family and my mentor were preparing me for my defining moment.

That defining moment came when a friend of mine called and told me his lease wasn't working out on Wall Street. Was I interested? Why not? The next thing I knew, I had an office on Wall Street, and it was time to get serious.

Firming up the Details

During those first few years while I was building my practice, I went to a workshop that taught me several lessons I still use today. My first "ah-ha" moment was the understanding that to grow, I had to create a firm instead of being a one-man accounting practice.

I was landing some good clients—like my wife's chiropractor—but I couldn't get in the door with the bigger clients because I didn't have a firm. I didn't have that level of credibility. So I got together with my former college mentor Alan Kahn and another CPA, Patricia Boyd, and we created Kahn Boyd Levychin, CPAs in 1994, which eventually became KBL.

The other important lesson I took from that workshop was something that struck me on a personal level. I started thinking about what defined me. I'm part black, part Jewish, part East Indian, and part Chinese. My family history has always fascinated me, but until now, it was simply that—a fascination—until I started to think about it.

I've always lived in diverse communities. For example: my neighborhood, Park Slope, where I've lived since my junior year in college, has one of the highest concentrations of lesbians and interracial couples in the country. When I started to think about it, throughout my life, diversity had punctuated everything I was ever involved with. It's part of who I am. The workshop was a revelation. It allowed me to see business as a community made up of diverse people and the benefit of creating a firm that honored that diversity. At last, I'd discovered the missing ingredient in my career and my business. Diversity. It was right there all along.

I'm what you'd call an accidental entrepreneur.

My business just showed up.

It was April 15th, 1986. I'd just finished my tenth busy season in public accounting, and I was exhausted.

Diversity has played a tremendous role in my firm's success. When we first started, we primarily did accounting, audit, and tax work. But as time went on, we chose to diversify into other services, including litigation support and forensic accounting, technology, internal audit and risk management, and outsourcing. Our client base diversified from individuals and small businesses to high net-worth individuals, emerging businesses, publicly held companies, and Fortune 500 companies located both nationally and globally.

Diversifying our service offerings was the main reason we were able to survive the global financial meltdown of 2008 and 2009. It's simple mathematics: the more stuff you have to sell, the better chance that someone is going to buy it.

The Importance of Mentors and Strategic Relationships

My partners and I made the decision early on to acquire minority-certified status, and that opened a lot of doors for us. What has happened over the years is that the larger minority-certified CPA firms have partnered with major, national firms so that they can leverage both firms' resources to pursue Fortune 500 and government contracts that embrace diversity. For example, the largest black CPA firm, Mitchell Titus, became a global member of the Big Four CPA firm Ernst and Young. Another large black CPA firm, Watson and Rice, has partnered with KPMG on many engagements.

We ended up making a deal with Eisner, the 25th largest CPA firm in the United States and the seventh largest in New York. We created a second CPA firm called KBL Eisner. We owned 51 percent, and Eisner owned 49 percent. It was a win-win situation. We had relationships within the Fortune 500, but we didn't have the size to service them. When we combined with Eisner's 600-man firm, we then had the size we needed, and Eisner gained access to the Fortune 500 through our client relationships.

Within this structure, we've worked with AIG, Citigroup, Genworth Financial, Goldman Sachs, J.P. Morgan Chase, Major League Baseball, Merrill Lynch, and UBS. Eisner's founder, Dick Eisner, became a mentor to me. Having a 15-minute conversation with Dick is like getting a masters degree in accounting.

There comes a point at which you can't just do what you've always done and rely on your skills alone. You have to become strategic, and you need mentors. I've been blessed throughout my career to have people like Alan Kahn and several of the partners at Eisner, along with a lot more people that we don't have space to mention, show up in my life to offer their wisdom, time, and mentorship. These are people who understand me, my heritage, and my focus, and they can advise me within the realm of who I am and what I want to build.

Creation vs. Harvest

One vital means to that end is this: You always have to be in creation mode in business. That's what makes it work long-term. Of course, you have to harvest what you currently have, but what I've seen happen in a lot of businesses is that they start off in creation mode, and then, when they get to a certain point, they switch completely into harvest mode and everybody else catches up to them, negating all of their advantages.

During those first few years while I was building my practice, I went to a workshop that taught me several lessons I still use today.

By the time they realize they need to get back into creation mode, they're behind the curve, and then they kick into panic mode. We have two rules for creation mode. The first is simply to develop more services to sell to more clients. There is a component of this called the cross-sell, which I'll explain later. The second rule is to be strategic. In other words, don't sell stuff that is off-strategy or off-brand (like a KBL clothing line, KBL Records, *KBL: The Broadway Play*, or KBL Airlines: "We Audit the Friendly Skies"). When we create, we're true to who we are.

At KBL, we're constantly in creation mode, meaning we're always looking to develop new services and products to sell to existing clients (the cross-sell) and also to sell to new markets. But these new services and products must match the firm's current DNA, strategically. For example, as I write this, we're in the final stages of acquiring a CPA firm that focuses on providing tax and business management services to the sports, entertainment, and media industry.

More diversity. The practice has several high-profile clients. We can sell the current clients of this practice our existing wealth advisory services, which generate additional revenue that didn't exist before—a combination of harvest and cross-sell.

We can also leverage the existing high-profile clients to get more high-profile clients in both the current tax and business management offerings (harvest), and we can provide audit, outsourcing, and a plethora of other services (cross-sell and harvest) to these new clients. Down the road, we'll develop (create) something new to sell (harvest) to these clients, and on and on it goes.

Playing the Game

Business is a game, and I love all aspects of this game. In my current role, I get to create our firm's identity and the strategies that will take us where we need to go. That includes creating the firm's branding, bringing in talent, identifying additional lines of services to offer clients, and bringing in business.

Of course, this industry has unique aspects, but a lot of its commonalities apply to other industries. Here are some of the larger lessons I've learned:

Lesson #1:
Cash is king.

Protect and follow your cash. Be strategic about how you spend it. Always know what your cash flow needs are and what they will be.

Lesson #2:
Work *on* your business instead of *in* your business.

In the beginning, you may have to hunt it, kill it, clean it, cook it, serve it, and eat it—whatever "it" is. This allows you to know every facet of your business. But for long-term growth, look to build critical mass from a revenue standpoint so you can delegate the harvesting part and free yourself up to engage in creative mode.

Lesson #3:
Always be lean.

Big dinosaur companies lose their creativity. They get fat, they get stuck in harvest mode, and they stop creating—or they create crap.

Lesson #4:
Don't wait until you need it to look for financing.

The best time to acquire debt is when times are good and you don't need it.

Lesson #5:
Always set aside time to be creative.

It could be at the gym. It could be in a yoga class. Or it could be while you're looking out the window. Wherever the place, it's in this creative space of the imagination that opportunities and possibilities appear.

Lesson #6:
Put your family first.

On a personal level, if an important meeting comes up on the date of your kid's school play or basketball game, re-schedule the meeting. Years from now, you'll still remember your kid's event. I submit to you that years from now, you not only won't remember what the meeting was about, you also won't remember who you met with or why—if you even recall having had the meeting at all.

Lesson #7:
Create your company to be a community.

Diversity has played a tremendous role in my firm's success.

When we first started, we primarily did accounting, audit, and tax work.

But as time went on, we chose to diversify into other services, including litigation support and forensic accounting, technology, internal audit and risk management, and outsourcing.

Make your company one that you would want your family to work in and extend this sense of community to your customers. This approach has worked wonders for me. My business is an extension of all of the diverse people who work in it.

Lesson #8:
Build brand identity.

Take time to discover who you are and create both yourself and your company as a brand. Sometimes people get fuzzy on what it is you do. For a firm like ours, that's constantly diversifying and transforming who we are and the services we offer, our core values can sometimes get lost. The way you combat that is to create brand identity that is foundational. That helps all the other pieces fit.

Jay-Z is one of the most well known entertainers in the world, but he also is an entrepreneur with several very successful businesses. One of my favorite sayings about brand identity comes from a Jay-Z song, and it goes like this: "I'm not a businessman. I'm a Business, Man."

I wish great success to all you entrepreneurs.

 Richard Levychin is CEO and Managing Partner of KBL, LLP, a 100-man CPA and Advisory firm with offices in New York and New Jersey. Richard has over twenty-five years of accounting, auditing, business advisory services, and tax experience working with both privately owned and public entities in a variety of industries. Richard is a member of the American Institute of Certified Public Accountants, New York State Society of Certified Public Accountants, National Association of Tax Professionals, National Association of Black Accountants, and Association of Latin Professionals in Finance and Accounting. He's been featured in a variety of business periodicals and conducts seminars on a wide range of business topics, including SEC matters and taxation.

The Hundred Book Rule

8

Breakthrough Training
Jeffrey Benjamin

They say that when you love what you do, you'll never work an-
other day in your life. That's Jeffrey Benjamin, and he shows us just
how important it is to have a love affair with your career. This story
is a walk through of year one of his business and the lessons he
learned. He shares them here, but more importantly, he shares his
passion to help others reach their goals and achieve personal fulfill-
ment. What is it that you love to do, and are you doing it?

—Ken

E very can I collected was a treasure, and I learned pretty quickly that anyone with a strong work ethic, passion, and perseverance could earn money. That's what got me through those cold mornings when it was snowing and the rubber bands I used to wrap the newspapers kept snapping in my hands. I knew I would succeed at whatever I did. The question was: What did I want to do?

I found the answer at age eighteen. I'd read probably a hundred books about personal achievement, but it wasn't until I read Napoleon Hill's *Think and Grow Rich* that my life's calling hit me. It was like I'd been slowly filling a glass for years until, one day, it was finally full, and I was ready to drink.

My mission was to help others reach their goals and to achieve personal fulfillment.

Youthful Ambition

At first, I got involved with a nonprofit organization that brought in motivational speakers. By the time I was nineteen, I was hosting meetings once a month with various speakers. It was great training for a teenager, but it was intimidating.

The first time they handed the microphone around for introductions, I darted out of the room, pretending I needed to go to the bathroom. But I couldn't keep using that excuse. They would've thought I had a bladder problem.

Eventually, I started getting out in front of people, grabbing the microphone, and falling flat on my face. And it wasn't just the speaking that was hard. I remember one handout I put together, one that was only about five pages. When I looked at it afterward, I must have found two dozen typos. It was embarrassing, but it didn't matter. I was still getting up and doing what I was passionate about. And as I did it more and more, my confidence grew.

A lot of executives I now deal with want me to do speech coaching with them for the simple reason that they haven't done enough public speaking. The only way to get better at something is to do it over and over until it's just like brushing your teeth. All that practice made me polished, and I really felt like I was ready to do my own thing.

But there was still one major problem: I couldn't book enough work. I knew a lot of people, and I thought for sure they'd hire me. These were close associates. I even did a mortgage for one of these guys while working at my "real" job. But when I met with him about speaking, he didn't want anything to do with me.

Not a lot of people were hiring twenty-three-year-olds to come and speak to groups. I had no problem landing the engagements over the phone, but when I'd show up, they were like, "Who the hell are you?"

Fortunately, I made a wise choice that I'd recommend to anyone thinking about striking out on his or her own. I kept my other job. As a mortgage banker, I was making good money, and I set my own schedule. Keeping that job allowed me to build my business slowly until, at age twenty-nine, I was ready.

The First Year

There were times during that first year of Breakthrough Training that I thought about going back to being a mortgage banker. I really thought striking out on my own was going to be easier than it was. The hours were long, the money wasn't good, and it was hard work landing engagements. I did a three-hour training session for someone that paid $1,750, and I thought, "Man, if I can do ten of these a month, I am cooking." But it wasn't easy to do ten a month. In fact, it was several years before I was doing ten trainings a month.

So my advice is, keep your day job, even though you may not love it. There is no such thing as an overnight success. If you don't plan to work your tail off, then don't be an entrepreneur. You have to be willing to carry two or three jobs. You have to endure sleepless nights because there is work to do, your debt is piling up, and your family pressures are mounting. I didn't want to keep my day job. I wanted to quit, pronto. But imagine two boats sailing different courses. Before you swim out to the other vessel, make sure it can carry you without sinking.

Lessons Learned

As I said, it's important to do something that matters to you. My business grew from a passion. I do it because I love it. I stay with it because I love it. Obsession creates its own motivational might. Successful people are successful because they fall in love with what they do or they do only that which they love. Challenges become insignificant when passion is involved. So find what pumps you up and resolve to make money doing it!

Aside from that fundamental and most important lesson, here are a few others I learned in my first year of business:

Lesson #1:
Ignore people who say it's impossible.

Once I announced my departure from the banking business, just about everyone told me in one way or another that I was crazy to walk away from an established, well-paying career. I never listened. Like the song says, "Nobody is going to rain on my parade." I refused to let anyone rain on my passion. Wilbur and Orville Wright did what others thought impossible. Columbus didn't sail off the end of the earth. Space flight wasn't just science fiction. The world is full of people who succeed despite the naysayers who discourage imagination and dreams. When someone tells you what you're doing is impossible, use it as motivation, not as a reason to quit.

Lesson #2:
Take a break to reshape, modify, or sustain your vision

I still engage in this vital practice. The constant barrage of information in your life can cloud your mind. The ability to escape to reflect on what is most important can be revealing. If a vacation is too great a time commitment, then take an hour, half a day, or a day or two to reflect. The point is to step back and clear your mind. Then record your thoughts and your feelings. They may be useful.

Lesson #3:
Select the right partner.

All sorts of chaos and challenges arise when we build relationships with the wrong people. I started out with a partner who seemed as passionate about personal development as I was, but for whatever reason, he couldn't maintain the same level of commitment as I did. Maybe he just didn't love it as much.

> *So my advice is, keep your day job, even though you may not love it.*
>
> *There is no such thing as an overnight success.*

I see this a lot in business. One guy is gung-ho, and one guy is ho-hum. Unfortunately, it can wreck a good friendship. Find a partner who doesn't stand between you and your goals. Find a person who supports you, a person with similar goals and values, whether that partner is a customer, vendor, spouse, employee, investor, co-owner, or a friend.

Develop a list of qualities you'd like to see in that partner. Then do your part to create the relationship. And be willing to part ways if it doesn't work. Circumstances change. Personal crises can alter a person's perspective and goals. And not everyone has the same mission in life that you do.

Lesson #4:
When you choose your partners, define roles and expectations clearly.

This is one of the things my partner and I didn't do. We didn't say, "You're in charge of sales and marketing, and I'm in charge of finance and program development." And it really cost us. To create a team that works well together, all the members must know and agree upon what they're going to contribute. Does everyone on your team know the goals and the measurable objectives? Does every team member know and understand his or her specific role? Don't make it an international mystery, and don't assume anything. Spell it out. It will save you many headaches.

Lesson #5:
   Be immune to rejection.

In my first year, I was sure most people on my target list would say "Yes" when I pitched my services. Most said, "No." The truth is that people will say "no" more often than they'll say "yes." Rejection can hurt, but that's no reason to give up. Rejection is part of being an entrepreneur. It's a good thing Edison didn't give up. It's been said that he tried 10,000 experiments before producing the incandescent light bulb. Then he had to work hard to get the public to accept his invention.

Instead of letting rejection depress you, let it fuel you. I'm celebrating my seventeenth year in business because I'm okay with hearing the word "no." I'm more than OK with it. In fact, I'm determined to turn those "noes" into "yeses." Some of those people who said "no" in my first year said "yes" years later because I kept asking.

Lesson #6:
   Know your numbers.

This may seem obvious, but I was terrible at this my first year. Every figure is important. Every lead and every conversion should be translated into dollar figures, and you should know the margin on your products or services. It really gives you a sense of the efficiency and success of your operation.

Lesson #7:
   Practice and improve your skill set every chance you get.

Confucius was right: "The expectations of life depend upon diligence; the mechanic that would perfect his work must first sharpen his tools." I read books, listen to authors, and take classes. The day you stop learning is the day you start dying. So keep learning and keep improving by whatever means you find most enlightening. For me, because I'm passionate about what I do, it's not work.

My first year in business was full of countless experiences and lessons—far more than I have shared. I think I've shed enough light on the pitfalls and areas of focus that helped me both start and grow a successful business.

I hope you go for it because it really is an amazing feeling to discover you can do just about anything you want—and make money at it—if you love it and put your mind to it. For me, having that epiphany was almost like seeing God. And it's one that I wish more people could have.

I was born an entrepreneur. And I was obsessed with personal development even as a child. The clues to what you love reside there—in your earliest days. I hope you find it, and that it becomes your life's work. The world will be better for it. Best of success to you, my fellow entrepreneur!

 For the last twenty years, Jeffrey Benjamin's focus has been sharing career and personal achievement strategies with individuals, youth groups, small business entrepreneurs, and Fortune 500 companies. He is the author of eight personal development books, including the book series *Real Life Habits for Success,* and has been featured on over 300 television and radio shows. Jeffrey is a speaker who has delivered more than 1,000 presentations in Asia, Europe, Latin America, North America, South America, and the Middle East. His Breakthrough Training™ produces positive results for more than 150 groups every year.

Moral Compass

9   Smartt Entertainment
Cindy Smartt

Serve first. That's the mission of Cindy Smartt, but until you read her story, I don't think you'll understand the depth of meaning that mission has for Cindy, a woman who saw the shortcomings of an industry and set out on her own to do things differently. She speaks of passion, but I believe her passion is for people—respecting them and caring for them. Even though she works in a high-pressure, high-profile industry with lots of egos, I find it fascinating that she speaks of peace. Her inspiration may ground her, but you'll find it's from a higher power.

— Ken

What's the most important factor in the success of your business? Passion. You must have passion for success in your work, your life, and your dreams. When you love what you do, work is easy. Who wouldn't want to spend the majority of their time doing things that bring them joy? That's what happened to me. I found my dream job. I actually get paid to work with some of the world's top musicians, actors, rock stars, and comedians.

As an entertainment producer for concerts at corporate and private events, I've produced over 300 headline concerts, including events for Bon Jovi, Journey, Carrie Underwood, Dancing with the Stars, Goo Goo Dolls, Alabama, Rod Stewart, Dana Carvey, Huey Lewis and the News, and Diana Ross. I've had the pleasure of producing shows internationally for artists such as Andrea Bocelli in Rome, Keith Urban in Sydney, Sarah Brightman in Barcelona, and Ben Vereen in Bermuda. I never aspired to do this job. In fact, until a concert company hired me, I didn't even know a job like this existed. But once I started the work, I knew I'd found my destiny.

As I became more and more successful in my job, I started to learn more about the business practices in the entertainment industry and uncovered some activities that were out of line with my values and my belief system. On numerous occasions, I was expected to compromise my ethics and even lie for financial gain. I was asked to not only stretch the truth about pricing restraints to the talent, but also to the client to secure more profits for my company.

I felt as though my loyalty and commitment were considered directly tied to revenue and not to customer service. It was a miserable way to do business. Sometimes when we're meant to learn a lesson, signs come to us in the form of whispers that we don't always hear. In time, these become louder until large red flags appear and our bodies force us stop and listen. At one point, I took a leave of absence from work due to stress-related health issues. When I stopped eating and my hair started falling out, I knew I had a serious problem. Those were my flags. As it turned out, although I wouldn't realize this until later, the less-than-ethical behavior of others did me a tremendous favor. I decided to leave my employer and be true to myself.

My Personal Inspiration:
I can do all things through Him who strengthens me.
—Philippians 4:13

I had no idea what I would do or where I would go, but I knew God was leading me to move on.

My first instinct was to market myself to competitive companies or event companies that could use my entertainment expertise. But in the process, when I reviewed my strengths, I realized that I already had everything I needed to perform the job on my own. I had the clients, I knew the agents, I could produce a show, I had the top technical producers in the world at my fingertips, and I had relationships with the best production coordinators in the business. I knew I could do the job, but could I run a company? I didn't know for sure, so I kept looking for a job. But every time I tried to become an employee again, I was led back to the same truth: I could do this on my own.

Unlike many entrepreneurs, I never dreamed about owning my own business while I was growing up or during my academic studies. My parents had their own company for thirty years, and I saw the long hours, the many problems with their employees, and their concerns about money, insurance, and retirement. That was not the life I had planned for myself.

But it was funny. As soon as I made the decision to go out on my own, I was at peace. I took a leap of faith because I knew that this was where God wanted me to be. It should've been the scariest time of my life, but it was one of the easiest. It defied logic on paper, but it was right in my heart. After that, things started to fall into place. Accounts I'd been trying to get for years started buying shows from me. One company that I'd been calling for four years bought their first show with my new company. Another client tracked me down to produce a huge concert at the Dallas State Fair Grounds for 5,000 American Airlines employees and guests. It was working!

It didn't take a lot of capital to start my company. Mostly, I needed to build a strong foundation by being protected legally, with the government and especially with my taxes. My top three priorities were hiring a lawyer to create client contracts and firm offers, bringing in an accountant to oversee my books and do my taxes, and opening bank accounts for my business to make sure my personal finances were kept separate from the business accounts. Falling short in any of those areas could cost me my business.

These strategic business investments came in very handy when my first deal almost fell through! The clients wanted to pull their offer to book the Pointer Sisters, which lead the agent for the talent to threaten legal action. I got down on my knees and gave this back to God. I knew He didn't bring me this far to leave me. I got a call back from the client a few hours later saying their lawyers had reviewed my documents, and they found them to be legally binding. My strong legal foundation and faith prevailed!

I needed very few material things to set up my office: a laptop, a printer/copy/fax machine, and two phone lines. I worked from my condo, sat on the floor in an empty dining room, and used a kitchen chair as a desk for my computer. In those days, I had to sit close to the wall since I had to plug into a phone line for dial-up Internet access. Spending money on advertising, slick marketing materials, and separate office space wasn't an option. I had a small, inexpensive brochure, stationery, and business cards. I don't believe in spending money that you don't have. I made sure I had the money before I spent it.

My Personal Inspiration:
"A journey of a thousand miles begins with a single step."
                                        —Confucius

My biggest obstacle was confidence. I was sure I was exactly where I was supposed to be, but I was afraid that the big agents for the artists—William Morris, CAA, UTA, etc.—wouldn't take me seriously. I also feared my corporate clients would feel the same way. As an employee, I used to have the backing and identity of one of the country's biggest entertainment companies, and I thought that was the only reason all of the big names in the industry and all the corporate executives were taking me seriously. Why in the world would anyone work with me alone?

One of my first phone calls was to Jay Leno's assistant. I called her to check on Jay's availability for an upcoming event and took the opportunity to let her know I had started a new company. I feared the worst. Her response stunned me. She was excited for me and incredibly supportive. She explained that there were other companies that had been taking advantage of Jay, but that she trusted me. That one phone call gave me the courage I needed to carry on. I was so excited!

That was the first in what would be many more encouraging conversations I had in the months to come. Not only did the agents and managers seem extremely happy that I was on my own, the majority of my clients also stayed with me. My new company had a great start with American Airlines, Gartner, Lucent, and GTE as clients.

What sustained and grew my business was my underlying practice of providing exceptional service. Although other companies often let the artists and the clients handle the details of the shows, my company is meticulous in making sure everything is perfect. Not only do we take care of their technical production, hotel rooms, transportation, and catering needs, we've also been known to work directly with the pilots of their private jets and run to the store to purchase socks and their favorite designer waters.

One of my biggest compliments came from the Four Tops' manager. He said, "You are the most professional company I've ever worked with. I've been doing this for forty years, do over eighty shows a year, and have worked with all the top corporate production companies. You are the best!" I was so surprised at his statement because I thought I was just doing my job.

Another reason my business became successful was my level of expertise in negotiating artist contracts and riders—documents that specify everything a performer and performance requires by contract. A rider can define anything from the type and amount of lighting required for a show to the specific type of candy bars the celebrity wants in his or her hotel room upon arrival. These documents itemize every detail of the show, and because it's an extremely specialized field, they must be handled with precision.

For instance, I met a potential new client who had just given an offer to Bon Jovi and didn't think they needed my services. They believed they were excellent business negotiators and that they could handle his contract along with his 54-page rider. They were wrong! In their desire to save money, they began to nitpick the requirements and made very amateur mistakes. Because it was apparent that they didn't know what they were doing, their original offer was turned down, and an additional $250,000 was added to the price. In essence, every dollar they tried to save cost them $100. After this happened, the client gladly hired me to produce their next six shows!

> *What sustained and grew my business was my underlying practice of providing exceptional service.*

I always go the extra mile. I believe you should deliver more than is asked of you. When a client is interested in an act, I offer to take the client to one of the artist's concerts or live performances and introduce them to the talent. At "The Tonight Show," our clients would always sit in Jay Leno's personal VIP seats and were invited on the set with him for photos. The practice of taking good care of both sides is a far cry from playing both ends against the middle. I believe that my loyalties are not only with the person signing the check. Everyone I come in contact with and every show I do is an audition for my services and an opportunity to establish my reputation.

My Personal Inspiration:
Trust in the Lord with all your heart, and lean not unto your own understanding. In all your ways acknowledge him, and he will make your paths straight.
—Proverbs 3:5-6

I never thought I would manage and own a multi-million dollar company. I was almost forty years old when I went out on my own. My passion for the job gave me the desire to take the chance. I love what I do! Now I manage my own schedule, treat people the way they should be treated, and am in charge of my own destiny.

Starting my own company should have been the hardest decision of my life, but it was one of the easiest! I stood my ground and walked away from companies and an industry that has historically treated clients, talent, and employees poorly. I had no idea what would happen to me, but I had an inner peace that everything would work out and knew that I was doing what God wanted. When you're doing what you're supposed to be doing, things fall into place.

You often hear it said, "Do what you love, and the money will come." For me, money was not the driving force. I didn't go into this business because it would make me rich; I did it because I love what I do. I have a real passion for my business, and it shows in the quality of my work. That's why I'm successful.

I believe that if you start a company just to make money, you'll never have the passion and the discipline it takes to be successful. It's just too hard. When you love your work, it doesn't feel like work, it's actually fun. Through my journey, I found my confidence, my passion, and my true identity. Do what you love, and your *peace* will come.

 Cindy Smartt, founder of Smartt Entertainment, has become nationally and internationally recognized as a top producer of corporate events. She's booked and produced corporate entertainment for leading corporations such as PGA of America, Allergan, Oracle, Lucent Technologies, Chevron, American Airlines, and Verizon, and produced more than 300 shows including Andrea Bocelli in Rome, Keith Urban in Sydney, Bon Jovi, Carrie Underwood, Jay Leno, Bill Cosby, Diana Ross, and Journey. Cindy received international recognition for development of her exclusive corporate programs featuring the stars and cast of *Dancing with the Stars*, *So You Think You Can Dance*, and *Top Chef*.

You're Fired! Now What?

10

M&E Painting
Matt Shoup

This story is proof that sometimes a part-time job isn't a part-time job at all. It's actually the budding business of a determined and sometimes desperate entrepreneur. Layoffs happen, and Matt was one of those casualties at his local bank. But what I love about him is that he moped for only a second or two, if at all. He quickly got on his feet, hopped on his ladder, and moved onward and upward. In his first year, he was tested, but day by day, he kept his perspective, gained clarity, and built confidence, which led to success. The saying is true: One thing leads to another. For Matt, a layoff led to the dream of starting a business and ultimately to long-term financial security. This is his story; it could be yours.

—Ken

"**H**oney, I'm home," I yelled after entering the door of my newly purchased condo. "I got fired today!" My battle to try and fit into the corporate world of mortgage banking was over. My new manager at the local branch told me, "Maybe you should stick to being a painter." My secure career was gone in an instant, and my future was unknown.

Trying to describe in words how I felt at the time is near impossible. I was flooded with fear, anxiety, anger, uncertainty, and defeat. Although these feeling were running through me, I was also filled with excitement to be free from the bonds of the corporate prison where I was employed. Now came the next step—what do I do now?

This is the story of my decision to become an entrepreneur, my frustrations along the way, the lessons learned, and finally, the successful results of my hard work and continued desire to pursue my dreams.

While I was attending college, my experience painting houses left me with connections to people who asked me to paint for them on weekends. While working as the mortgage man at a local bank, I'd do a few painting jobs on the weekend to earn extra income. Life was great, and things were looking up. I needed the extra money to pay off some debts and to start securing my young family's future.

Now, thirty minutes after being fired from the bank, I sat in my condo, defeated yet anxious to take the entrepreneurial leap. In March of 2005, I said, "Let's do this," and I moved forward with my painting company full-time.

I founded M&E Painting and opened its bank account with only $100. I had no savings and no investors. I just had a motivation and determination to pursue my dreams and support my family. On top of that, we'd just purchased a condo with "no money down" (the wonderful 105 percent financing), and I had large student loans and drove around in a car I couldn't afford. I was scared to death.

Our first fear was the fact that we had no money—either personally or in the business. The fear of where we would find money to pay for business bills as well as pay down our personal debts was one of the scariest things we'd ever experienced. To deal with this, we took a look at our personal budget and decided which things were needs and which were wants, both personally and professionally. My wife was a lot better at this than I was, and her insight and discipline helped us to stay afloat.

I should point out that my wife didn't enter our relationship with debt. The loans and car payment were mine. We made sure we were tight on our spending and didn't splurge on spur-of-the-moment desires. We saved a percentage of profit from our jobs to pay taxes, and we also packed money away for the slow winter months and in preparation for the following business year. The second frustration I had during the first year of business was with people telling me I was too young or inexperienced to do what I was doing. I was not the guy with thirty years experience (I was only twenty-three), but I was determined to make my customers

100 percent happy with every aspect of our company: the product, the service, and the follow-up. I had more on the line than other guys who had been in the business thirty years.

My first "ah-ha" moment was when I realized that when I had a negative situation or objection in front of me, I could turn it into a positive to win business. One example was when I was doing an estimate for a family and they mentioned that they were nervous about my lack of experience. This was an objection I faced a lot. They'd received competing proposals from two other painters who had been painting longer than I'd been alive. With this family, I finally overcame the objection. "I know they have been around for thirty years, and I'm sure those other companies will do a great job," I said. "But where will they be in fifteen years once I've made a name for myself? The only way I can do this is for you to trust me and hire me. Would you help me make a name for myself? You'll not be sorry!" I built such confidence in myself that I was able to overcome just about any negative objection and secure business.

> *Once I realized how to overcome objections and turn negatives into positives, I realized this didn't just apply to selling jobs and earning business.*
>
> *I could use that skill in every aspect of business.*

I knew that if my customers were going to hire me, they had to trust me. I used to my advantage the fact that my new entry into the painting business meant that I was either going to make or break it on their home. If they hired me, they would be putting a huge amount of trust in me, and that trust meant the world to me. I told potential clients that I wouldn't let them down. How much motivation did the guy with thirty years experience have? Not as much as I did, I assured them. I was the hungry guy just breaking into the biz.

Once I realized how to overcome objections and turn negatives into positives, I realized this didn't just apply to selling jobs and earning business. I could use that skill in every aspect of business. When I was looking for potential employees, the perceived negative of my company not being well-known or well-established was outweighed by the vision I created for potential new team members to grow with us. Today, some of those original team members are leaders in our company.

After completing our first year in business and finding out that we actually did well at it, we were relieved that we were able to sustain our company and ourselves without needing to rely on anyone else. By the end of 2005, we weren't worrying about where our next check was coming from and could make lemonade out of any lemon you handed us.

We had a solid business plan and model in place. This included an organized system and procedure for handling incoming leads, selling jobs, and managing painting crews. While I was out selling jobs and managing crews, my wife worked on the administrative and accounting duties of the business behind the scenes. We turned an immediate profit, and throughout 2005, we identified the key metrics we needed to grow and scale the business in the upcoming years. These metrics included sales averages, closing rates, gross profit margins, return on marketing investments, and identifying when we would need to hire new team members for the office, painting, managing, and sales positions. We also had rave reviews from our customers and were becoming well-known for some of our out-of-the-box marketing efforts.

We were now ready to start growing the business little by little. We were both confident in our abilities to run the company and began to move forward with more drive and determination. With this confidence in place, we set bigger goals from the year prior and were filled with joy and excitement to be able to attain them.

One of our greatest memories about the early days of growing a successful company was going back to the bank that fired me in 2005. I never had any animosity or hard feelings toward them. My personality just didn't fit into their corporate mentality, and it was only a matter of time before I would've chosen to leave or else been fired. In 2008, we outgrew our home office and began looking to purchase a commercial unit. We had a large down payment, but we needed a loan to carry the rest. We shopped a few banks, and the one that had the most competitive rates and service was the bank that had fired me. I remembered them saying only three short years earlier, "Becoming a painter might be a better option for you." I guess it was!

It was exciting to show the vice president of the bank our personal balance sheet, as well as the books for our now multi-million dollar company. At this point, we were free from the worries we had in 2005. We were free from car and school loans, and had completely paid off our house. It was amazing to look over the corporate desk at the bank and show the bankers that we'd created our own success.

Keeping perspective is important in business and in life. During my first year in business, I thought I had the biggest problems in the world. The job that didn't go right, the upset customers, the employee we needed to fire, and more. These things kept me up at night, but in the big picture, they weren't big issues at all. Looking back on my first year, I realized the problems I had experienced then were miniscule compared to the ones we face today, and the ones we face today will be nothing compared to the ones we'll face five years from now.

Today, my concerns are our sustained and continued growth and scalability over the coming years, raising capital, and retaining earnings to grow. Both 2008 and 2009 raised concerns about the economic forecast and how we would weather the storm. Now, seeing our growth of 25 percent in revenues this year puts me at ease. Today, my financial concerns are not about being able to have my next paycheck, but rather to cover the payroll of our entire forty-five-person team.

As I look forward five years, I know my immediate concerns will be dwarfed in comparison to the concerns I'll have then. As you grow your business, you'll always be concerned about not just your personal viability but also that of your team members, whose paychecks you sign. Growing and sustaining your business in varying economic conditions, as well as capital concerns, will be issues that entrepreneurs can look forward to as their business matures.

Every problem has a solution. It causes stress at the time, but if you let that stress get the best of you, you can't go out and run your business the way you should. Don't stress. Remember that in five years, you may not even recall your current problem or will look back and laugh about it. Use today's problems to learn and grow. If the problems are due to mistakes you made, learn from them so that you don't make the same mistakes twice.

If you're a new entrepreneur, you'll find there is nothing like jumping out and deciding to run your own company. I experienced many fears and frustrations in doing this. It was one of the scariest things I've ever done, but while doing it, I was so filled with passion, enthusiasm, and excitement for what each new day would bring that these emotions cancelled out the negatives. Positive thinking and visualizing my success were my keys to doing well. I told myself everyday that I was the greatest, and I became stronger because of it.

When you run your own business it's easy to get sidelined when something bad happens and then to let those feelings plant seeds of doubt in your mind. I know from experience that before long, it's easy to believe your own doubts and watch your business begin to spiral downward. I overcome this by saying, "I'm the best at what I do. Nobody will stop me from attaining my goals. Sure, there is a problem today, but I will handle it with a positive attitude."

After all my experiences, lessons learned, ups and downs, joys, tears, and excitement, here is where we stand as of today: After starting with $100 in the bank and being in debt up to my eyeballs, M&E Painting has grown to become a multi-million dollar profitable company. We're the best-known painting contractors in Northern Colorado and are now expanding statewide. Our brand is known throughout the community for our superior quality, craftsmanship, and service; for being one of the best places to work in Northern Colorado; and for being very active in giving back to the community. Our company is close to becoming debt-free, and we have a clear vision and laser focus for where we're headed. My family and I are completely debt-free. Our financial lessons learned along the way have allowed us to change our family's future. We'll be able to provide for and support our children and their children by growing our assets and accumulating wealth.

I've also learned that I'm pretty good at this business stuff. Other companies have sought my advice, knowledge, and expertise in business, which has led me to create my second company, Shoup Consulting, LLC. My goal is to inspire other entrepreneurs and help them with their entrepreneurial journey.

 In 2004, Matt Shoup founded M&E Painting, LLC with only $100 in the bank. M&E Painting is now a profitable multi-million dollar company and Northern Colorado's largest painting contractor. Sharing experiences with other entrepreneurs is a passion for Matt. He created Shoup Consulting to help entrepreneurs implement effective strategies and systems to grow their companies. Matt also teaches Spanish at a local elementary school and created the Matthew P. Shoup Study Spain Abroad Scholarship at Colorado State University.

Rejection as Part of Success

11

Water Babies
Dan Lauer

Too many would-be entrepreneurs cave in at the first hurdle. They can't take criticism, and they let roadblocks stop them. They have an idea and want others to bring it to life for them because doing it for themselves is too hard. Dan Lauer is the exact opposite. He is a true entrepreneur, and his resolve and resiliency—along with business sense, as you'll come to see—are why he was so successful with Water Babies, as well as his more recent ventures. When you read his story, you'll understand that a good idea will get you nowhere without follow-through, and Dan meticulously spells out the proper follow-through. Want to make sure your product lands on store shelves instead of collecting dust in your basement? Then read this chapter…often.

—Ken

If I told you that my pitch for what I hoped would be a best-selling toy involved a latex glove with a fake rubber head, would you think I was either pulling your leg or a few cards short of a full deck? If I told you that same strange "prototype" led to the second-best selling doll in history, would you laugh at me?

Therein lies the first lesson of being an entrepreneur: You can't care what people think. You can't be afraid of ridicule and failure. And you can't be daunted by humble beginnings—or you'll never succeed.

When I first tried to sell the idea of Water Babies more than twenty years ago, I wrote more than 700 letters to toy manufacturers, and I got more than 700 rejections. I even got a certified cease-and-desist letter from the legal department at Hasbro telling me to stop badgering their chairman. My mom cried when I told her I was quitting my banking job to pursue my idea, and my in-laws wouldn't invest in it. Still, I never gave up.

I was like a relief pitcher in baseball. If you get clobbered and blow a save one night, the very next day you still have to get right back on the mound with your head on straight. There's no denying that the entrepreneur business is fraught with uncertainty, anxiety, risk, and rejection. It takes a person with resolve in the face of obstacles and resiliency in the face of setbacks. A lot of entrepreneurship is white-knuckle driving, and a lot of the effort leads to failure. Yet regardless of the results, pursuing the entrepreneurial dream is still worth taking the chance because you already know the downside. What you don't know is the upside.

Childhood Inspiration

When I decided to make a go of Water Babies in December 1989, I didn't have an actual prototype to market to potential investors or distributors. What I had was a childhood memory. When I was growing up, my sisters' favorite toys were dolls that they made out of balloons. They filled balloons with warm water; taped them together to form the head, body, and limbs; drew on a face; wrapped a blanket or a cloth around their creation; and cuddled it as if it was a real baby. My sisters loved them, and I never forgot it. So I used balloons to build the first Water Babies.

To create the best prototype I could on a budget, I experimented with different materials, including yellow latex gloves, hot water bottles, and even condoms—testing their various strengths and suitability by dipping them in latex. I'd thumbtack the water-filled materials to my countertop like test subjects. And yes, I took them all, even the condoms, to meetings with various toy manufacturers and investors.

As zany as the idea and the prototype might have seemed, my idea was sound. The companies I presented Water Babies to actually liked the concept. They didn't reject me because of the crudeness of the prototype or because they didn't think the idea of a cuddly water-filled baby doll wasn't a good one. There was something more.

From rejection, I learned a very important lesson: Don't shut down when people say, "No." Instead, listen intently to their reasons. Because I heard "no" a lot, I had a lot of opportunity to understand what I was missing. What I heard over and over again was that my idea, while good, was not proven. So I went back and worked on proving the potential of Water Babies.

I should tell you that Water Babies wasn't some fly-by-night idea that I decided to pursue on a whim. The idea and the product were well planned. I'd been successful in the banking industry for ten years and had some credibility and practical business knowledge when I began. Right from the start, I treated Water Babies like a business in which everything was about time and money. I hired myself to work ten hours per week

> *From rejection, I learned a very important lesson: Don't shut down when people say, "No."*
>
> *Instead, listen intently to their reasons.*

at $10 per hour, literally putting in $100 a week as an investment for six months while I researched whether this idea of creating a water-filled doll was viable.

At the time, I didn't know anything about dolls, and the Internet wasn't around yet, so I couldn't just perform a quick search. Instead, I walked into ToysЯUs, looked at the back of boxes for toy manufacturers' names, and called to get their companies' annual reports.

Knowing the players was just one spoke on the wheel. What about intellectual property or patented trademarks? What about competition? What about distribution? I wanted and needed to learn the whole wheel of business, but in a balanced, risk-free way. I didn't quit my job as a bank vice president until I was certain I was going ahead with this project, and that meant having a product that had a chance at success.

Today, people come to me on the brink of divorce with their basements full of games that are virtually identical to something I can find at ToysЯUs, and they ask me for help. What can I tell them? They ought to have done their homework. It's not what they want to hear, but it's the truth, and it's what they need to hear so that they don't make the same costly mistake again.

Research is vital. Water Babies wasn't the first idea I explored, but it was the first one for which I felt there was a real market. Thus, it was the first in which I invested real time and money. After taking calculated, gradual steps for six months, I performed another research check, and the dolls still made sense. There was no water-filled product available, but Cabbage Patch Kids and Pound Puppies were exploding. There was clearly a big market for cuddly toys. This was an entrepreneurial avenue I could explore.

My goal was to have Water Babies be a best-selling doll within three years. So I asked myself, "What must I do to go from this big idea to that big result?"

Tipping Point

In the spring of 1990, I decided to produce 5,000 dolls and sell them in St. Louis as a test market. I hired a doll sculptor to design the doll, I met every week with a board of advisors to discuss what we were doing, and I raised $300,000 in seed money during the first quarter of 1990. As an entrepreneur, it's really important to know what you don't know. You can't have founder's dilemma—thinking you're the smartest person in the room—and be successful. I knew I needed to hire the best lawyer, the best PR firm, and in my case, the best doll designer I could find.

It wasn't like I was an expert in this field. I'm a typical American male. What did I know about girls' dolls? I leaned on a lot of people for advice and expertise. Not surprisingly, there were more hurdles ahead.

When you're an entrepreneur, things move quickly. You can't account for everything, even if you have the best peripheral vision. Here's an example of a big hurdle that hit us hard as we tried to get Water Babies off the ground. Just as we were preparing to take the toy world by storm, our first production run had a rejection rate of seven out of ten dolls. What made matters worse was that we'd already shipped the dolls to stores. They were about to hit the shelves.

Within a period of about three days, I had to contact all the stores and switch out the entire product line—and do it without alarming anyone!

Of course, I ran out of money, so I had to raise more. It really is true when

> *It wasn't like I was an expert in this field, anyway.*
>
> *I'm a typical American male.*
>
> *What did I know about girls' dolls?*
>
> *I leaned on a lot of people for advice and expertise.*

entrepreneurs tell you that it will cost twice as much and take twice as long as you expect to be successful. You just can't account for all the variables you'll face.

What got me through that painful setback was a big poster of a rollercoaster that I kept on my office wall. I looked up at it one day and said, "Oh, I must be in one of those dips." Then I realized that it's horrible when you're flying down the hill and you can't stop. But if you don't crash and die, you're going to come up again. My roller coaster poster told me so. And we did.

On the Friday after Thanksgiving, a regional retailer, Venture, allowed me to demonstrate my product at their stores. I had pretty women and moms handing out these warm, cuddly dolls to chilled, mitten-clad little girls outside the store. That was my tipping point. The kids loved them. From there, the sales and publicity exploded, and the chairman of Venture called me to say he wanted every doll I could get him.

All of a sudden, I was in the papers, making headlines like "Banker Gone Bonkers." I was on the morning radio shows and television talk shows, showing off my dolls and enjoying the best kind of marketing—free. My goal had been to sell 5,000 Water Babies in five weeks. Instead, we sold more than 15,000, and we had orders for 60,000. I couldn't manufacture or ship them fast enough to meet the demand.

What I didn't know at the time was that Venture and Wal-Mart were whispering to Mattel, "Help this kid out. Buy this thing."

With our mini-success of 60,000 units, and no way to deliver them, I flew to Hong Kong to attend an international trade show and some meetings. Not just any meetings, though. These were real meetings with the industry's top brass. There I was, hobnobbing with the president of Mattel, the chairman of Hasbro, and the chairman of Playmate Toys—veritable titans of the industry. And they called me! How did that happen?

The answer is simple. I'd proven the potential of Water Babies.

It was amazing how the tables turned. These major manufactures got into a bidding war for the license to produce my product, and I set what I considered a very big goal of 350,000 dolls in five markets. Once I chose Playmate Toys, the makers of Teenage Mutant Ninja Turtles, that goal changed. We hit a home run, shipping 2.2 million dolls representing over $30 million in sales in eight months.

The Broad View

When I look back on all we've accomplished, I feel a great sense of pride and achievement. The success of this product has given me the credibility and brand recognition needed to pursue other ventures. It's also provided financial stability for my family and endless opportunities for my children.

The facts that 20 million Water Babies have been sold, and that 20 million girls grew up with Water Babies, are really cool. It tells me that our vision was right— that we hit on something very basic and instinctive when we created these dolls.

I was walking through the Dallas airport recently and saw a little girl carrying a Water Baby. It made me smile. I was talking with our team recently at a restaurant, and the waitress told me a story of how she had a Water Baby as a child. I was touched. It's really a dream come true to have that kind of impact on the world. But the reality is that no one is going to make your dream come true for you. And even if someone did, it wouldn't be worth it.

A lot of times, inventors will come to me and say, "Make my dream come true. I don't have any time. I don't have money." What I want to tell them is, "If it were that easy, a lot of people would do it." It's not that easy. It's hard work. And sticking with it through the ups and the downs is what separates those who try from those who succeed.

On the flip side, there are a lot of people out there who are willing to help you. It's true. So, if you're a new entrepreneur, don't be afraid to bounce your ideas off others, to seek help, or to ask for money. Find bright people and lean on them.

There's a saying that success has many fathers and failure is an orphan. There are a lot of people today who take a lot of credit for Water Babies, and I don't care. Let them. It's important to make room for all those people on the boat, and it's important to enroll them in your vision. That thought dovetails with my primary purpose in writing this chapter, to share with you the two most important qualities an entrepreneur must have: resolve and resiliency.

When I speak of those two traits, I'm not talking about an arrogance that says, "It's got to be me because I'm always right." I'm talking about a steely resolve that lets you know you're going to see this thing through no matter what happens.

There were tremendously tense moments in the birthing of Water Babies and plenty of hurdles along the way that literally could have stopped me in my tracks. You would've never heard about me, and you would've never heard of Water Babies if I had let those hurdles knock me out of the race. But, whether you live to be fifty, seventy-five, or 100, I believe it's worth pursuing your wild idea and proving it, because you never know where it might lead.

To every entrepreneur out there with a wild idea, trust in your genius, trust in yourself, and do something. Start small. You may succeed or fail, but you must try. Use your best talent and resources, and take your ideas seriously. But the idea alone isn't good enough.

> *Business is not that easy.*
> *It's hard work.*
> *And sticking with it through the*
> *ups and the downs*
> *is what separates those*
> *who try from*
> *those who succeed.*

Put a plan around it, and build a business case. Prove that wild idea, and make it un-wild. And more importantly, make it profitable for you and those who buy into your vision. The effort is worth it, and my experience tells me that success takes a measured approach.

Water Babies will celebrate its 20th year in continuous distribution in the fall of 2010. To celebrate, we're on the path to not simply inventing but to proving another idea. Watch for B My Baby Nursery in a shopping mall near you. The best is yet to come for you...and us.

B My Baby

Dan Lauer is the creator and licensor of Water Babies, the second-longest and second-bestselling baby doll on the market. His experience of moving from undiscovered inventor to the creator of Water Babies as a top-selling classic is chronicled in *Forbes, Inc. Magazine, Fortune Small Business, People, Entrepreneur, Commerce, The Washington Post,* and *The New York Times*. In addition, he's been featured on CBS "Morning," CNN-fn, and CBS's "How'd They Do That?" Dan has led several start-up companies and not-for-profits, and is a licensing agent, keynote speaker, and consultant to the consumer products industry.

From Classroom to Boardroom

12

Idapted
Adrian Li

When you read this story, consider this point: Learning in the class-room is only the beginning. Real learning takes place the minute you step out into the real world of entrepreneurship. In the real world, your teachers are your customers, your potential investors, and your network of business contacts. Adrian and his partner Jon-athan had the best educations money could buy in the classroom, but it still didn't fully prepare them—even with their A+ business plan—for the roadblocks, the landmines, and the hard work it takes to get a real business off the ground. What I love about their story is that they kept finding new paths and new people to help them make their dream a reality. And they discovered that the passion for their dream and their ability to inspire others as true believers made all the difference.

—Ken

You could call us a textbook start-up—literally. My co-founder, Jonathan, and I met as students at Stanford University. We were both interested in educational technology, and we were both accepted into "S356: Evaluating Entrepreneurial Opportunities," a highly sought-after class that delivered the best simulation of starting a business in the real world.

In that class, you built a team, developed a business idea, and wrote a business plan. It was excellent training. But for Jonathan and me, the class was by no means *just* a class. For us, it was the prerequisite to our future. It was the first step to accomplishing our dream of starting a business in education technology.

After two hectic weeks of networking and courting candidates for our team, we managed to bring together the best of the best. We landed a consultant with experience at McKinsey; a marketer with experience at Clorox; a student from the Learning, Design, and Technology school; and a student who knew the ins and outs of a start-up operation. Dream phase one was ready to go.

Over the next two semesters, we worked hard on our business plan. Top mentors from Stanford guided us as we followed a carefully designed curriculum and meticulously covered every aspect of our plan. In the process, we learned the importance of flexibility.

As we developed our plan, we ended up completely changing the initial idea. Our plan was to teach people languages online, but we'd missed one critical ingredient in our original concept: speech training. Thankfully, a market research project led by our consultant and marketer team members brought this to light, and we adjusted our plan to allow people to connect and practice their new language skills.

The research told us even more than that, however. We thought that people who spent time on language learning sites did so to learn. Not so. We found that a large motivation was social interaction. The research discovered that people would rather pay for results, and didn't want to risk talking to a random person. They didn't care if the other voice on the line was a certified teacher. A trained native speaker was sufficient. This was valuable information, and our dream took shape—a little differently than we had envisioned—but it took shape nonetheless. Now we just had to turn our passion into something that could actually make money.

As if the world of technology and labor were aligning around us and for us, two trends were colliding like a perfect storm: The growth of broadband Internet access and a large number of highly educated people who wanted to work from home. What could be more perfect? Companies such as Jet Blue and LiveOps were pioneering a model known as a "virtual call center" to tap into this pool of labor and deliver high-quality, low-cost call center services.

We figured our company could hire our trainers and have them provide one-on-one oral English training to thousands of students based in China, right from their spare bedrooms, home offices, or kitchen tables. We could use the virtual call center model and custom-built technology to empower work-at-home moms, dads, students—you name it—to be highly effective language trainers.

There it was! We could provide highly effective, highly flexible English language training to Chinese students at a fraction of the cost of face-to-face teaching. It was a perfect solution for a desperate market—at least in theory.

We spent weeks on research, presentations, and financial models, and by the end of the course, when we finished our presentation, our professor ranked us among the very best teams. This plan was a winner, and we knew it—we could feel it. Surely someone would see the huge potential in this idea! After all, China, with its huge aspiring middle class and high propensity to spend on education, was the largest market in the world for our service. This idea couldn't lose.

Our A+ business plan satisfied our course requirement, but if we were going to actually turn it into a business (two of us decided to make a go of it), we needed money. From that point forward, we entered a different classroom—the classroom of bottom lines, experience, and results.

We knew from our plan that the capital we required to make our dream a reality was far more than any amount we could get through a loan or a credit card. Even though language training is a people business, our service required technology. That meant we needed to invest in the research and development of a highly-integrated, Web-technology platform. That was the only way we could effectively deliver and scale our service.

The First Sell...

We weren't experienced in raising money, but we knew enough to understand the odds weren't in our favor. We'd always hoped we'd find one investor who saw the light, was as passionate as we were, shared our excitement, and wanted to get involved. But deep down, we knew better. Even if we found someone who believed in our idea, there were a few things working against us. Neither of us had started a formal business before, although Jonathan had already successfully designed and sold an online shareware product while at the university. But that was a far cry from our current ambition.

For this venture, all we had was our business plan and our dead-set belief and passion that our idea would revolutionize English language training.

Potential investors care more about the team getting a business off the ground and building it than they do about a great business plan. They care about who will execute a great idea more than they do the great idea itself. They want to know whether the team has relevant experience. They ask: Are they experts in the industry they're entering?

Even though we were passionate about our idea and felt we had the business figured out on paper, we knew we could benefit from the help and advice of people who had been there before. Fortunately for us, we had a head start with a seasoned investor as our mentor, Russ Siegelman of KPCB. He guided us in terms of general business. But we also needed some people with operational experience. Without that, it would take far too long to put the essential parts of the business together.

Lesson #1:
Work your contacts!

What we quickly learned was that searching for advisors was our first real-world lesson in selling our dream. In the beginning, when you have nothing, you and your team are everything. Knowing how to sell our vision and matching it to our audience—in our case, prospective advisors—was crucial to getting them onboard. We would have to inspire them if we expected to get anywhere. So our first step was to look at the people we already knew. Why start developing new contacts when Stanford afforded us a pretty good network already?

We contacted the professor who had first introduced us to the virtual call center model. After all, he inspired our direction in the first place. After we shared our idea with him, it didn't take long for him to recommend just the person we needed to meet. Within no time, he introduced us to Bill Trenchard, then the CEO of LiveOps, the largest virtual call center in the world. Not a bad first contact. Our goal for meeting Bill Trenchard was simply to learn as much as we could about the virtual call center model.

> *Our A+ business plan satisfied our course requirement, but if we were going to actually turn it into a business we needed money.*
>
> *From that point forward, we entered a different classroom—the classroom of bottom lines, experience, and results.*

There we were: A couple of students, wide eyed with entrepreneurial aspirations, looking to do research into an idea. But something happened as we began to share our vision, our research, and our plan. Bill's eyes began to engage too. When we told him that language students valued native speakers the most to help train them, he really lit up. His entrepreneurial spirit came alive as he clearly realized the huge potential of the virtual call center model to teach English to Chinese people. He saw how he could help. We inspired him!

At the time, LiveOps was screening tens of thousands of applicants for its work-at-home sales and support jobs. Bill immediately realized that LiveOps was turning away many applicants who were not necessarily qualified for sales and support, but who could be great trainers. Wouldn't it be wonderful to create a work-at-home opportunity for them as well? By the end of the meeting, he told us, "If you guys go out and build this, I'll put some money in and be your advisor." That was a win!

Lesson #2:
   Get potential advisors excited about how their own experience can immediately benefit a new business, and they'll be more inclined to be involved.

After that meeting, we continued to identify the areas in which we needed to strengthen our knowledge and experience. I attended an education conference at Stanford and went to a seminar given by Bob Xu, one of the co-founders of New Oriental, a $2.5 billion market capitalization, English-language training company. I was fascinated by how New Oriental had persuaded millions of students to learn English. During the presentation, Bob spoke of the challenges that these students faced and how New Oriental trained its teachers to meet the students' needs.

Afterwards, I was able to arrange a dinner meeting with Bob through the Greater China Business Club and got to know him on a more personal basis. We were able to seek advice from Bob, who later expressed interest in advising and investing in us. Another key resource was a leading English language training expert at Stanford named Dr. Phil Hubbard. Not only did Phil specialize in computer-assisted language learning (CALL), but he also had experience working with a start-up business delivering asynchronous (training on the student's—not the teacher's—schedule) English language training to students in Japan. Our passion was spreading. We were sharing the potential, and it was paying off.

Our confidence in our idea grew with every expert we contacted. We kept connecting to people and establishing our advisor base. We knew we needed every advisor we could find. We identified our knowledge gaps and filled them with experienced advisors. We didn't know anything about virtual call centers; so we brought in the leading authority who did. We didn't have on-the-ground experience in China; so we brought in the co-founder of the most successful English language training company in China. We didn't have education expertise; so we worked with an expert in the field to develop our training approach.

Even after we raised our seed funding and started executing our plan in China, we didn't stop looking for valuable advisors to bring on board. Later, we also brought in the founding engineers from Skype. Who better to advise us about our voice over IP service (VoIP), an Internet-based calling system, than the VoIP experts?

We even added one of the leading operators on the Internet in China to our team. We were more than willing to put in all the hard work on the ground, but we needed the advice from experienced professionals to help reduce the number and severity of the mistakes we were inevitably going to make.

The Second Sell...

We now knew we'd sell the vision and the plan. We had a solid team of advisors, many of whom said they would invest, but we also needed more capital. If finding advisors was the warm-up, then the next phase of selling the vision was the big game. We needed experts to lead the round of investment. Based on the early-stage nature of our venture, we decided that rather than pitching to venture capitalists who used pools of capital, we would be better off approaching angel investors or groups, individual investors who use their own money.

Angel groups were more willing to fund small amounts of money like $500,000, and angel groups were more likely to take a passive role after the funding. We didn't need the distraction of highly involved investors. We turned to our network of advisors for introductions to potential angel investors and groups.

In no time, we had a dozen introductions to potential investors—not a huge number of leads. We knew that we needed to make the most of every one. The meetings came in different forms. Some were as casual as getting coffee in a café. Others were part of an entire dinner at which we were matched up against other entrepreneurs looking for funding. But no matter what the surroundings were, the key was to deliver a short, clear, and concise pitch.

One of the biggest concerns the potential investors had was with our understanding of the market. They'd never invested directly in companies in

China before, and for all but one investor, this represented too great a risk. But one opportunity was all we needed, and we had the opportunity to pitch to a group called the Sacramento Angels.

Sacramento Angels was a small but professional group of investors, and many had been through the trenches of Intel's formative years. They were smart people and looked for early stage ideas that needed capital. Prior to our pitch, we rehearsed our presentation countless times. We compiled a video demonstration of what the service would be like, and we prepared supporting documentation for our business idea.

The group decided to take a chance on us. They had never invested in any company based outside of the U.S. before, but, with the advisors we had backing us, Jonathan and my combined experience, and the potential of our business idea, they were willing to put around $300,000 into helping us get the company started. That was a win for our idea, a win for our plan, and a win for our dream!

> *One of the biggest concerns the potential investors had was with our understanding of the market.*

The Real Sell...

Getting our advisors and funding in order was great, but we knew our hard work was just beginning. Everything we'd been through was just the dress rehearsal for the new challenges that every day would present to us. But through all of those challenges, our commitment to our vision, each other, and our advisors drove us forward. Everyone who helped us along the way believed in us, and, most of all, they showed us that we could believe in our idea and ourselves.

⑦ldapted

Adrian Li is co-founder of Idapted, the largest provider of live on-demand, one-on-one language instruction. Prior to starting Idapted, Adrian worked for Pepsi in project management in Shanghai, JPMorgan in London advising on acquisition and growth strategy for financial institutions, and Globalegacy, a social enterprise incubator advising entrepreneurs who are starting for-profit social ventures. With a passion for education, Adrian founded a UK-based charity, CNY Trust, that raises money to support children's education in rural China, provides scholarships, and has built a primary school in the village of Da Miao, China.

Mentor Your Way to Success

13

Fairytale Brownies
Eileen Spitalny

Sometimes in the early days of a business, it's a good idea to keep your goal quiet. People might think you're crazy if you tell them the truth about what you believe. If you're young enough, they'll pat you on the head and say, "Isn't that cute." But by the time you're out of school, a goal like creating the Best Brownie in the World might sound a little ambitious. This was the case for Eileen and her partner David—especially since they weren't trained pastry chefs. This story just goes to prove that the best and the most successful entrepreneurs are undaunted. Once they get an idea in their heads, very little can stop them.

—Ken

When my business partner David Kravetz and I decided to create Fairytale Brownies, the one thing we knew for sure was that we wanted to bake the best brownies in the world. It was a simple goal—or so we thought. It was 1992, and we were just twenty-five years old. We knew next to nothing about owning our own business or baking brownies, and we didn't know our dream of baking the best brownies in the world meant starting a manufacturing and direct marketing company. We had no idea what we were getting ourselves into, and maybe that was best.

David and I met in kindergarten on the school playground in Phoenix, Arizona.

I don't remember the initial play date or conversation, but it was enough fun to cultivate a lifelong friendship. I know one thing—our first get-together definitely included a plate of his mom's brownies.

Her brownies were a behind-the-scenes part of our formative years. A plate of brownies always rested on her kitchen counter, waiting to be devoured by everyone who walked by. As we grew older, David and I discovered that we made excellent partners on school projects. Starting in third grade with pixilation animation, we continued working together on school projects all the way through high school physics. I visualized the big picture—the "where we're going with this"—and David knew exactly what formula was needed to make that vision materialize.

In high school, David and I talked about owning our own business together when "we grew up." I'd say, "I'm in charge of demand, and you're in charge of supply." It was a classic economics model that we eventually realized we wanted to recreate, with brownies as our product. We went our separate ways for college, but we were only an hour's flight away from each other. He went to Stanford and majored in mechanical engineering. I went to the University of Southern California and majored in business and Spanish.

During my days at USC, I worked in the Entrepreneur Program. There, students had access to the Advisory Council and its members' real-world advice. It was in that program that I learned the importance of asking for expert help. With our business still in mind, I told David that when we launched out on our own, we would always ask for expert help, and eventually have a board of directors. I saw how experts supported and helped the students, and I never forgot how valuable that experience was in managing a business.

A few years later, both David and I graduated and joined the corporate world. I took a job for a Spanish television network in Phoenix. David went to work as an engineer for a large consumer packaging company in Cincinnati. We wanted to get some professional training and "real-world" experience in management, marketing, processes, and HR. We learned some good and bad skills to apply (or not apply). We also saved money to support us in our first year of business.

I did well in my sales position, and David made a great engineer. But after almost six years, I was still itching to be my own boss, to create something on my own. David was, too. So without delay, David proposed to his girlfriend, moved back to Phoenix, and asked his mom for her brownie recipe. The recipe was free, and we were on our way.

I'd like to say that the first thing we did was jump in with both feet, rent a retail space, buy a mixer and an oven, and start baking brownies. But it wasn't that dramatic. We were too pragmatic. The first thing we did was write our business plan. The second thing we did was save enough money for one year's worth of living expenses. Did I mention we're both realists?

From there, while still employed, we started asking for advice. We showed our business plan to a friend who was a local manufacturing plant business owner. He said, "It looks great. But get rid of your credit card debt before going to the bank and asking for a loan." We took his advice, paid down our debts, and then went to the bank for a loan. We must have looked like eager kids with our business plan in hand, our college degrees, and our naïveté. The banker kept looking around the room as if expecting someone else—and he was! He was looking for our co-signer.

Needless to say, we didn't get a dime for from the bank that day, and in the end, our parents co-signed for us. But just one short year later, we got our first SBA loan. That got the parents off the paper, and from that point forward, David and I have been on our own as 50/50 partners.

That first year was one of sacrifice. And so were years two and three. One of our advisors who owned a mattress spring manufacturing company told us to start thinking and acting like a Fortune 100 company if we wanted to be successful. "Be ready for where you're going before you get there," he said. It was great advice, but it meant paying ourselves very little, putting everything we had back into the business, and picturing ourselves right up there with Godiva Chocolates, Ben & Jerry's Ice Cream, and Harry & David.

At the ripe old age of twenty-six, I cashed in my 401(k) so that my boyfriend (now my husband), Mike, and I could pay the rent. He was our baker at minimum wage, and David and I weren't getting paid so that we could put every dollar back into the business. I didn't even have health insurance. That wasn't smart. Don't consider that worthwhile advice.

Believe it or not, you can act like the "big guys" even when you don't have much money. Thinking like a Fortune 100 Company wasn't all dreaming. We started to create systems—systems we really didn't even need at the time—and processes, too. For us, that meant product consistency. "That's what the big guys really have," we thought. So we went without, we scrimped, and finally we were able to buy our first piece of machinery, our brownie-cutting machine.

We bought that first machine with a credit card with zero interest for six months. It was like free money! And we just rolled it over to another credit card offer, and so on and so on. The cutter helped with production because it guaranteed a consistent 3"-x-3" brownie. Not only did it speed up our process, but it also made our product look more legitimate. Consistency of experience is key when it comes to any brand.

In the beginning, consistency was there for our budding group of customers, but efficiency wasn't there for us who were working behind the scenes. We had no baking experience, and it showed. We baked brownies at night in a friend's catering kitchen after working our day jobs. We baked a couple of pans and then we'd sit outside and wait for them to cool. If they weren't perfect, we threw them away. To us, product consistency was our customers' first impression. There was no room for error.

When I think back, I realize how much time and product we wasted waiting "to see." We should've been making another batch while we waited. But then again, what did we know about baking?

One thing we did know was that there had to be a better way. So once again, we asked for help. We asked anyone who would listen, and that included family, friends, neighbors, and local small business outreach services.

Beth, the daytime pastry chef at the catering kitchen we were using by night, steered us to an importer so that we could find the very best chocolate for our brownies. She also told us we were going to make it—that she believed in us. She had no idea how encouraging those words were.

> **Believe it or not, you can act like the "big guys" even when you don't have much money.**
>
> **Thinking like a Fortune 100 Company wasn't all dreaming.**

We were in over our heads, but we weren't willing to give up. Batch by batch, we experimented with chocolates from all over the world. I took plates marked "A" and "B" to my coworkers at my day job and asked which brownies tasted better. I told them that my friend was thinking of starting a brownie company and needed some true opinions. Of course, they eventually realized my "friend" was me. My "taster clients" later became loyal Fairytale

Brownies customers.

It's hard to pinpoint one particular thing that was the toughest part of our first year. There were so many challenging (I mean, learning) moments. Everything we did that year was new, and we had to make so many important decisions, often very quickly and without a lot of information. That year, we learned we had a "fourth quarter" business that we had happened to start during the fourth quarter. We didn't know our business would naturally be seasonal and that we'd happened to start it "in season." Consequently, when we opened our doors, we were really busy. "Wow!" We thought, "We've got a hit on our hands."

What we didn't realize was that the fourth quarter is the busiest time of the year for gift giving. Naturally, we were busy. But then our first summer arrived. As the thermometer climbed, our sales sank. We realized two things: We sold and shipped chocolate in Arizona. Not smart. Shipping chocolate brownies in 112-degree weather isn't good. Thankfully, the first problem was easy to solve using David's engineering know-how. We quickly learned about air packs, ice packs, and insulated boxes. But then came the second realization: We didn't really have anything to ship in our wonderfully insulated packaging. Apparently people don't buy many gifts in the summer. Now what?

A triumph came out of that summertime hardship. Here we were with more brownies than money, and because we had no money to advertise, we sent brownies to food editors at newspapers and magazines. hoping that they would love Fairytale Brownies as much as we did. Amazingly, *The New York Times* wrote about us in their Dining section in June of that year! In the food world, that's like getting the golden ticket or winning the lottery. That article brought us enough business to get us through the summer.

With more sales and an inefficient production system, we still had a big problem on our hands. We decided it was time to get a little baking consulting from a real pro. We found an expert who taught us a quicker baking procedure, which we loved. She also showed us ways to cut corners using different ingredients and skipping some baking steps. At first, we thought this was great, but it soon sank in that taking the cheaper route was not the direction for Fairytale Brownies. Remember, our goal was (and is) to offer the best-tasting and number-one brand of brownies in the world.

That was a big lesson for us. Expert advice is always valuable, but you don't have to take all of the advice you get. Some of it may not be applicable to you, and some of it is even bad. Today, I still ask for advice, and if more than one expert says the same thing, it's probably worthy of a try. But the ultimate test is my gut instinct.

We solved most of our production challenges and became more efficient. After we achieved a level of success that afforded us the ability to market our brownies, you'd think it would have been smooth sailing. If only that were true. One year, we ran out of brownies during our holiday season. There was no catching up either, no matter how hard we tried.

Even though we were primarily a mail-order company, we always had a small storefront at our bakeries. People could walk in and buy family and corporate gifts, and we'd often get very big orders—certainly in the hundreds of dollars and sometimes even in the thousands of dollars or more. Here was the problem: We had loose and very speculative inventory controls along with thousands of prepaid orders from our direct-mail customers. We had to fill those orders before we could take new ones. So, right at the peak of the holidays, we had to limit the number of brownies we could sell in our store.

This was painful, particularly when our customers could look behind the counter and into our production facility and see brownies stacked upon brownies. We had no excuse except that we were new, and that's what we told our customers. Those brownies you see, we told our storefront customers, are already promised to other customers. Most understood, but it wasn't fun disappointing people, no matter how understanding they were. A few people were not happy at all, and that really was tough because we knew they would likely tell everyone they knew how unhappy they were.

In business, particularly when you're a hands-on entrepreneur, it's always something. One day, we arrived at the bakery to discover that someone had cut all the telephone wires by our back door. Not good for a mail-order company. Another time, our landlord forced us to move into a larger location in the shopping center where we first started. The larger space was wonderful, but he made us move during our busiest time of year. We were wiped out physically and mentally. Then the landlord's movers dropped our mixer. That was the icing on the proverbial brownie! And then there was the unfortunate Valentine's Day when we arrived at the bakery and found that someone had thrown a rock through our front window. Although nothing was stolen or damaged (except the window), it was another challenge and another expense. All these inconveniences were lessons in disguise. From that point forward, we got smarter about everything, including lease negotiations.

As an entrepreneur, you'll face challenges day after day. But when you own your own business, you're so passionate about what you do that you somehow get through it all. You work eighteen to twenty hours a day and don't mind because your passion keeps you going. What seems like a big deal one day becomes just another problem to solve the next. Best of all, it's thrilling to see your creation grow before your eyes.

But other things can suffer during these exciting times. My weight went up and down in 10-pound increments. Sometimes you just forget to eat, and sometimes you eat too much—especially when you're making brownies.

Your family may never see you. Being an entrepreneur was my dream, not my husband's. The idea of owning my own business excited me, not him. But I was asking him to trust me even though I didn't know what I was doing. Thankfully, my husband supported my dream even when we had no idea what would happen next.

I also neglected outside activities, even the things I loved. Going to dance class, practicing yoga, and working with nonprofits went by the wayside.

The good news is that a healthy, well-designed business can eventually provide the best of both worlds: the entrepreneurial thrill and the balance you and your loved ones need and deserve. I've found that the freedom, flexibility, and successes of owning my own business far outweighs the trials and tribulations—and it's way better than working for someone else.

It's actually quite exhausting to recollect all these memories because I remember how tired I was when it was all happening. But interestingly, even while in the moment, the thought of quitting never once occurred to us. Maybe you feel the same way I do. Once you see your business and employees growing, you never want it to go away. You pour yourself into the business, overcome the challenges, and celebrate even the tiniest of successes. Each hurdle you overcome is a company success, a milestone. And in the process, your business reaps the benefits and becomes that much stronger and more valuable.

When David and I began our business, we wanted to create something special and memorable. Seeing how everything has unfolded over the years, it's definitely a fairytale come true.

Eileen Spitalny, along with childhood friend and business partner David Kravetz, turned a dream of entrepreneurship into Fairytale Brownies, a gourmet mail-order company that ships more than 2.5 million brownies a year. The company now has annual sales of more than $9.3 million and has been featured in *Edible Phoenix* and *Life & Style Weekly*. Eileen is involved in Entrepreneurs' Organization, Arts & Business Council, and Arizona Women in Food & Wine. She was named the USC Alumni Entrepreneur of the Year in 2002 and Arizona's Small Businessperson of the Year in 2006. Eileen is also featured in the cookbook *Cooking with Les Dames d'Escoffier: At Home with the Women Who Shape the Way We Eat and Drink.*

Your Business is Right in Front of You

14

Understand.com
Darik Volpa

As you continue your journey as an entrepreneur, you'll learn what Darik learned so clearly. Reality bites in business. What I really like about Darik's story is how he bites back, time after time. Even at a crossroads in his life, he decided to bite back rather than cower— meaning he saw an opportunity, and he grabbed it. Through it all, he provides a very clear set of rules created from lessons he learned through the trials and tribulations of being in business for himself. All are a testament to his success, and all are worth posting on your wall.

—Ken

It will cost more. It will take longer. You will sell less. After reflecting on my first year as an entrepreneur, which started in the summer of 2003, these three statements best summarize the advice I'd give anyone who is about to start a business. Also, I'd recommend having a supportive spouse (if you're single, that's even better) and a prescription for Ambien to help you get through the tough parts.

"But," you may say, "I have a well thought-out business plan, and I've spent countless hours doing my research to reduce my risk and ensure success."

To you I say, "Uh huh."

"And if I only get 1 percent market share by the end of year one, I'll have a wildly successful business."

"Right."

At some point, nearly every entrepreneur has used that same formula. My business plan had over forty pages of dribble with multicolored graphs and a glossy cover. It was useless the day I started selling my product. That plan now resides deep within a filing cabinet, waiting for the day my friends and colleagues want to publicly roast me.

Lesson #1:

Talk with as many people as you can about your idea. The more people who can help you vet your idea, the better. Don't get caught up in non-disclosure agreements or keeping the idea a secret. Most people have no intention of copying you and will offer valuable insight. The value gained from others input will far outweigh the risk of someone stealing your idea.

Let's go back to the summer of 2003. I was thirty-three years old, recently married, and coming out of a successful sales and marketing career at Stryker Corporation, a $7 billion orthopedic device manufacturer. Over the course of my career at Stryker, I'd launched fifty medical devices and managed more than $50 million in products. I'd taken an important product line that was losing market share and turned it around, taking it to an industry-leading growth rate by introducing new products and a revamped marketing plan. I was recognized with numerous awards, including Marketing Professional of the Year. I felt like a marketing rock star!

The celebration was short lived, however. I was shocked and in disbelief when I learned I was bypassed for a promotion to lead the marketing department and would now report to a former roommate who'd been named the new Director of Marketing.

That event, coupled with simultaneously watching one of my closest friends sell his business for $38 million, inspired me to start my company, Understand.com, a year later. Little did I know that *not* getting that promotion was the best thing that could have happened to me, both personally and professionally.

Lesson #2:

When things are darkest and you're at your lowest point, you're more open to new opportunities and risk taking. My friend who sold his company for $38 million had interviewed with Stryker years earlier and was turned down for the job. He then decided to do his own thing, which in turn led to his tremendous success.

I think back and laugh now, but at the time when I was passed over for that promotion, I felt like I'd been punched in the gut. My options were to remain in my current position, accept the decision, and be a good soldier, or to resign and look for a new job. As I prepared my resignation letter, I reached out to a former mentor at Stryker to get his advice. That conversation convinced me to stay with the company and relocate to a new division in Boston.

The lasting effect of not getting the director position was profound. Reporting to someone else and having him control where I went, what I did, and what I earned was no longer palatable. One day, after several months into the new job, I'd just finished an exceptionally long period of travel and trade shows during which I'd worked fourteen straight days, and needing to reconnect with my wife, I decided to take her to breakfast. When I arrived at the office, instead of saying "Thank you" or "Nice job," my new boss reprimanded me for coming in an hour late! This incident proved to be the final straw that pushed me to take action. I felt like Neo in the movie *The Matrix* taking the red pill and awakening to a new reality—very soon, I would own my own future and become an entrepreneur.

With this new reality, each problem that I encountered looked like an opportunity to start a business. While I went through the motions at Stryker, I found myself distracted with crazy ideas and a burning desire to make bold moves. I was on a flight from Boston to San Jose when I really began to coalesce my thoughts about what would become Understand.com.

> *I was confusing activity with productivity.*

As a salesman in the medical field, I was always searching in vain for material to educate myself on orthopedic procedures so that I could talk intelligently with doctors. Either the material I found was geared to surgeons and far too advanced for me, or it was too simplistic and provided little educational value. I'd also painfully watched doctors and patients try to interact during consultations. Surgeons may be skilled in the operating room, but they're often not good communicators. Patients usually had poor health-care literacy and were nervous, often forgetting to ask important questions. There was clearly an opportunity to bridge this gap. My idea was to create 3D animated movies that surgeons could license and put on their Website to better educate patients.

Lesson #3:
Stick with what you know to improve your odds of success. The industry insight and connections that you have will prove invaluable when you go out on your own.

For several months, I worked on my idea late at night and on the weekends. In hindsight, far too many hours were spent crafting the perfect business plan and creating detailed PowerPoint presentations. I was confusing activity with productivity. I should have spent more time thinking about global opportunities, scalability, and additional ways to monetize content. These initial missteps limited our growth in the early years.

In May of 2003, I submitted my resignation to Stryker and moved to tax-free Reno, Nevada to start Understand.com. I hadn't spent much time in Reno, but it turned out to be an excellent decision, both personally and professionally. I wanted to give myself every opportunity for success, and starting the business in a state with a favorable tax climate and lower cost of doing business made sense.

Lesson #4:
If you're prepared to do whatever it takes and your business has the flexibility to move, consider tax-friendly states like Nevada or Texas. The money you save will mean more money to reinvest in the business. Additionally, if you plan to sell the company or have some other liquidity event, you'll keep significantly more of your money.

For the first year, I worked solo out of my home. The logistics of starting the business were invigorating, overwhelming, and scary. I dealt with funding, LLC creation, operating agreements, patent submissions, credit card processors, business licenses, opening bank accounts, Website development, and product development. On top of this, I was a sales and marketing guy with no technology background who was liquidating my savings to start a tech company. In hindsight, I'm surprised there was not an intervention from friends and family.

Lesson #5:
The greatest risk most entrepreneurs will initially face is insufficient cash flow. Be absolutely insane about keeping your expenses low. Work out of your home. When you need office furniture, buy it used. Use contract labor as much as possible. Use tools like Skype and Gotomeeting.com. By minimizing expenses, you give yourself

more time and the luxury to make mistakes—something you'll do often.

In September of 2003, Understand.com launched its first product. In my brilliance, I'd forecasted a stretch-goal of 500 surgeon sales by the end of the year. After all, I was a brilliant marketer and an amazing salesperson with a strong understanding of the market. The prospects of instant success seemed reasonable.

When December ended, I found myself a mere 493 sales short of my goal. I had enough revenue to cover my long-distance phone bill.

If it weren't for a sincere belief in my idea, a supportive spouse with a good job, and the prospects of a very public failure, I may have reconsidered my decision. While the possibility of crashing and burning was real, I simply couldn't imagine going back to my former lifestyle. As long as I was breathing, this endeavor was going to play itself out.

In June of 2004, I got my first big corporate sale. It provided much-needed capital and traction for Understand.com. That sale consisted of a large lump sum along with significant recurring revenue to fund future growth. To this day, that client remains a great customer and a key supporter—it was my former employer, Stryker. They once again played a pivotal role in my life.

Lesson #6:
When it's time to leave your employer, do it with class, no matter your feelings. Make sure you flawlessly hand-off your responsibilities and make yourself available to answer questions after you leave. Having an axe to grind is juvenile, and it may come back to haunt you. You never know who your customers will be.

Over the years, my business has flourished. We've moved out of my home and now have a fantastic office complete with a game room, sun deck, basketball court, and showers for those who bike to work. We have thousands of doctors licensing content from around the world and boast a corporate client list that would be the envy of any company. In July of 2009, we opened our first international office in Brazil and have plans to open other international offices in 2010.

Is it less stressful now? Not really, although the stress is different and far more manageable. Do I have regrets? None. Would I do things differently? There are always things you wish you'd done differently, but those missteps are now a part of my DNA and will help me make better decisions in the future. Do I wish I would've become an entrepreneur sooner? No. I cut my teeth in the corporate world and had a paid education for nine years that served as the foundation for my business. I remain grateful for the opportunity I had at Stryker and think about those experiences and relationships with great fondness.

Lesson #7:

Rethink the traditional monetary measure of success. Money will not make you happier. Yes, it's cliché to say that, and it will mean little until you become "rich" (which is completely relative). In fact, money may make you less happy, more suspicious, and more worried that you'll lose it. What money will do is provide you security and give you more options if you manage it correctly.

My final words of advice: The decision to completely own your future can wreak havoc on your psyche. There're no scapegoats when you're an entrepreneur. The convenient excuses many people use in the corporate world mean little when you own "it." You've heard the excuses before: engineering designed "it" with the wrong features; the FDA didn't approve "it"; the sales team couldn't sell "it"; or manufacturing made "it" with the wrong material. All of these reasons, real or imagined, ultimately mean little when "it" is all yours. When it comes to your own business, you're the one who achieves or fails. Good luck, my fellow entrepreneur, and Godspeed.

Darik Volpa is Founder and CEO of Understand.com, an Inc. 5000 company and global provider of health-care content that helps patients better understand conditions, procedures, and diseases. In 2006, Understand.com was awarded "Best of Show" at the Silver & Gold Venture Capital Conference. Darik gained much of his experience at Stryker Corporation, a $7 billion medical device company, where he managed more than $50 million in products and was responsible for the development and launch of over 50 medical devices. He was named the 2007 Innovator of the Year by *The Business Report* of Northern Nevada, and in 2009, received the *Reno Gazette Journal*'s "20 Under 40" award and was named a "20/20 Business Visionary" by *Nevada Business Magazine*.

The Journey *Is* the Success

15

Uniguest
Shawn Thomas

It's common to hear people talk about their "success journey" when they describe what it took to achieve one goal or another. But for many entrepreneurs, Shawn among them, the journey is the success. When you read Shawn's account of his life before Uniguest and during his first year, you'll understand the subtle difference. You'll realize that entrepreneurs seldom have an end that lasts. There's always something else, something bigger, something more challenging that lies ahead. There's always another journey.

— Ken

Y ou might say I'm an entrepreneur out of the need to survive. I have no college education and no formal business training. But I do have lots of passion, and I strive with perseverance. I started my current company in 2002 and, at that time, I was about as broke as you could be. My car had been repossessed, my mortgage company was calling me every month threatening to foreclose on my house, and I didn't know what to do. I've learned over time that being an entrepreneur is risky stuff. (I wish I would've known how risky fifteen years ago.) What got me into that financial distress, which is not uncommon for new entrepreneurs, was trying virtually any and every type of start-up business that I could find. From network marketing to this and that, I spent almost a decade and every penny I had (and didn't have) trying to find my calling.

I started Uniguest through pure passion and salesmanship. I had an idea, and I was confident that it was something that was going to come to fruition. Nothing was going to stop me. My idea was simple, which was good because simple is easier to sell.

Uniguest serves the hotel industry and provides guests access to things like the Internet and business applications through our technology products and services. We also provide access to destination information through pre-printed city guides, restaurant menus, directories, and more. I've learned that people like access. That's why the Internet is such a phenomenon, right? When you can help people find the information they need, you become highly valued. And it doesn't matter what shape the economy is in.

Initially, I started with one product and worked out of my almost-foreclosed-upon house. When I started the company, I had no idea where I wanted it to go. Initially, it was just a means to an end. I didn't have the luxury to think much about it. I needed to make some money, and I hoped it would turn into something bigger.

During the first year, I was able to pay myself a little bit. I managed to keep my house and get a car, but by no means was I living large. I thought that if I could just make $150,000 a year with my business, I would be "successful." In the first year, I made a lot of mistakes. The biggest one was that I didn't find any mentors to help guide me. It took me a good eighteen months to see the light.

On the other hand, it didn't take long to learn that while I liked the freedom of business ownership, being alone and working from the house was not really that much fun. What I liked was selling, but of course, that was only part of my job. I had to run a business too, and that meant understanding accounting, human resources, legal issues, and most importantly, people. It became apparent that the bigger the company got, the more I had to learn about being a leader and manager. Over the years, it was my business partner, a seasoned entrepreneur, who taught me the "people" side of the business. He was a great teacher.

While I highly recommend talking to individuals who have been around the block, I can tell you that success is within your reach regardless of your background—if you focus on the right things. My belief has always been that sales drive everything. As long as I or someone else in my company is selling and driving revenue, the rest will take care of itself.

Realistically, I know now there is a little more to it than that, thanks in part to my mentor. I still remember the day that I first met him. (He later became a business partner). He helped me transform my company from a home-based business with $250,000 in annual revenue into a company that today is bringing in $10 million in revenue annually. Uniguest now has seventy employees, and I've far surpassed my goal of $150,000 a year in income.

People often ask what has been the toughest part of building Uniguest. Honestly, it's not something I can convey with a single story. For me, it's that the destination is never something

> *I started Uniguest through pure passion and salesmanship.*

that I can actually achieve. For me, the definition of success is continually changing, and the pursuit of success is like a journey. I review my own individual desires and goals, virtually every day of every month of every year. And then those goals change. My initial goal might have been to make $150,000 a year when I first started, but now my goal is much, much higher than that—and it also includes giving back and developing an exit strategy with large upside potential. Success is a moving target with no real end.

But despite the challenges, the entire experience of being an entrepreneur has been extremely fulfilling. Over the years, we've had some amazing celebrations, not only financial wins but emotional wins, too. Our success has allowed us to do more for our community and the people within it. Through scholarships, fund-raising, and various charity drives, we've made a positive impact on those around us. And it took a while, but my business can now support others, not just me.

It's a great feeling to help people less fortunate than me.

As an entrepreneur, I'm at my best when I trust my gut instinct. Whether it's hiring, firing, investing in an idea, investing in a person, or trying something new, I always trust my instincts. I've trusted my gut about what relationships to invest in and which will not produce. I've used my gut instinct in deciding which employees to keep and which to let go, something to this day I find difficult.

As I look back at the first year that I started Uniguest, remembering those times is a bit cloudy. I've come into contact with many of my friends from times past. My address book has turned over many times during the last six years as we've grown as a company and I've grown as a person. The saying "birds of a feather flock together" is very true. If you're like me, you'll find your newfound levels of success will force you to develop new relationships with people and companies with which you'd have never thought you would be associated. Some good and some not so good.

Yet, I've always stayed rooted to my beliefs and my integrity. By doing so, I know the rest will take care of itself. The world is bigger than me and will go on when I'm gone. But as I've reconnected with some of my friends from the days when my company was new, it is absolutely amazing to think about how far we've come. Friends of old are always a reminder of where you've been and how far you've come. The life of an entrepreneur is very different than most. Most people have "jobs" and resist change. Entrepreneurs love change.

When I started my company in 2002, I was broke, destitute, and not sure where I was going. But because of my perseverance and a passion to learn how to grow a company, we're now sitting on top of the world.

Today, I think about how the definition of success has changed for me over the years. I've come to realize it's a journey, not a destination. And the true vision of it comes from within. I'm not a billionaire and don't have aspirations to be a billionaire at this moment. My journey is continuing, and my definition of success continues to morph. But I'm not restless. I'm happy to be running a profitable company, and I'm happy for the people with whom I work. Most of all, I'm just happy to be alive.

uniguest™

After starting out in the music industry, Shawn Thomas decided that would not be a lifelong career and he wanted to get out of it. A string of sales jobs and a failed business followed, providing tough lessons along the way. Shawn is now CEO of Uniguest, a multi-million dollar company with over 2,500 customers, 4,000 self-serve kiosks, and 70 employees. Uniguest provides print, technology, and specialized services internationally for hospitality, healthcare, and other industries. As for Shawn, he looks forward to challenges, new-found successes, and most of all, continuing to learn from his mistakes.

Carpe Diem: Seize the Day

16

Hire Quality
Dan Caulfield

Dan is a true American hero. Not only because he is a former Marine Corps officer, but also because he's made it his lifelong mission to help American military personnel make the leap from service life to civilian life. That mission isn't always easy, particularly in wartime. Veterans aren't always welcomed as warmly by businesses as they should be. Dan's story about his first venture is one of undying commitment to his men and women—the ones he commanded and the ones he didn't. It's the story of disappointment that led to a silver lining called The Armed Forces Support Foundation and HireAHero, a free community job service for military people and their families. If you ever wondered if successful entrepreneurs have a higher purpose driving them, read this. Then ask yourself, "What's my higher purpose?"

—Ken

Have you ever experienced an epiphany, a moment of complete clarity, understanding, and purpose? Mine came on a Friday morning when I awoke to the sound of the doorbell. I'd been out carousing the night before, and the only outfit I could manage to put on was a pair of boxers, a T-shirt, and a classic case of bed-head. I lived in one of those street-front apartments in Chicago, so, when I opened the door and took a step out, I was literally standing at the street's edge in all my undressed glory.

My unexpected visitor was the FedEx man. It was my first FedEx package, so I was excited. It made me feel important. I was scheduled to start my MBA program the following Monday at the University of Chicago and assumed it was something from them. It wasn't, but little did I know the package was a harbinger of the future.

I knew a lot about FedEx's business because I was very passionate about entrepreneurs, and Fred Smith, the founder of FedEx, happened to be a Marine Corps officer like me. His success, as well as the success of many other Marines who became entrepreneurs, was a big reason I became a Marine officer too. I saw the Marines as a great way to gain the leadership experience I needed to become a great entrepreneur. I've always felt it was my life's calling to be an entrepreneur. And there I was, in my skivvies, holding a package delivered by a company founded by one of my Marine-turned-entrepreneur heroes.

I quickly opened it and found a check for $3,000. It was payment for helping an employer find a Marine to fill a challenging position. To me, I was just doing a favor for a few guys in my platoon who had called me from a pay phone and asked if I could help them find jobs. They were all leaving the Corps but were terrified about what the civilian world had in store for them. These were men who went bravely into war, but transitioning from the Marines to civilian life had them scared out of their wits.

I was undeterred and certain this was my destiny. That very day, I went and ordered business cards.

On the check was a yellow sticky note from the employer that read, "In the real world, people get paid to do this. They're called head hunters." It was a life-changing moment. It was as if the hand of God had reached down and touched me. Suddenly, the whole world opened up, and my path was laid out before me. I was going to start my own company and help military people find employment through an Internet-based service.

It was the summer of 1994, and I used a BBS (Bulletin Board System) called Monster Board, which eventually became Monster.com, to help my Marines get jobs. We used the Internet in the military extensively prior to the launch of Mosaic, the first Internet browser. I knew I could copy FedEx's model—bring all the "packages" to the center, sort them, and send them on to their final destinations— for helping Marines find jobs. My packages were going to be people leaving the military, and the destination was going to be open jobs all over the world. Unlike FedEx, I wouldn't need trucks. I had a better tool: the very young Internet.

My reverie didn't stop there, though. I resolved to sell the company by 1999 to either Fred Smith or Ross Perot, another military officer who'd became an entrepreneur. Then I'd retire and never work again. The entire plan unfolded in my head as I stood there, barely dressed, on that Chicago sidewalk. Eventually, someone ripped me from my street-front fantasy by leaning out a window and screaming, "Put some [expletive] clothes on!"

I was undeterred and certain this was my destiny. That very day, I went and ordered business cards. The name of my new company was Hire Quality, Inc. I never showed up for my MBA program. My thinking was, "I'll hire MBAs."

Basic Training

The military is a huge organization, and the people within it learn, train, and master an incredible set of highly developed skills. Hire Quality worked for employers that wanted to hire military people, and the company grew from my back bedroom to over $1 million in revenue in the first year.

The military is a mystery to those who've never served. Often it's difficult for people to make the connection between military training and experience, and civilian job skills. At the highest level, the military is just a big company with a specific mission. A vast majority of the jobs and responsibilities are the same as any company, but it's very hard to get a job after leaving the military—especially for the young enlisted people who make up 80 percent of the 225,000 who transition from the military to civilian life annually.

The public absolutely identifies military personnel as having certain traits. You'll hear them spun as positives, but in reality, people perceive them in a negative way. For instance, people will say, "Military personnel are disciplined, and they follow orders." What that means to many people is really that military personnel are mindless automatons. The truth is that many of the skills that are most valuable to me today I acquired as an officer in the Marines.

For example, in the Marine Corps, you have to communicate very effectively to get people to buy into your vision and do what you want them to do. When you're standing out in the desert with a bunch of Marines who are holding dangerous weapons—tough young men, some of whom are former gang-bangers—you can't be the loud-mouthed, white-boy barking nonsensical orders. In a flash, you could get shot and be left for dead. Nobody would ever know what happened. As a military leader, you have to get your men and women to believe that what you are asking them to do, whatever the mission, is in the best interest of the unit and therefore in their best interest. That's why Marines perform their heroic acts. It's an unconscious consensus that what's being asked or ordered, in the context of the mission, is the right thing to do. Can you see how this applies to business?

The Green Room

While we were getting Hire Quality, Inc. up and running, one of my partners was attending an American Legion event in Tennessee when he called me and said, "You won't believe who's speaking here. It's Fred Smith!" I literally dumped out the quarter jar to pay for a rental car and drove all night to make sure I was standing in the green room when Fred Smith walked in. I worked it all out in my head on the drive down. Fred would walk in, I'd deliver my pitch about Hire Quality, its mission, and how we could help FedEx hire former military personnel, and we'd be in Shangri-La.

There was one problem. Fred was up on stage pitching the World War II Memorial. He never came into the green room. All of my plans were blown. But I wasn't about to let the opportunity slip away, especially after driving all night from Chicago to Tennessee. After the speech, I saw Fred walking toward the front door, but I couldn't get to him while he was shaking people's hands on his way out. I looked at my partner. He looked at me, and then I just took off running out the door. Fred was already in a limousine when I got outside, so I jumped into the car and sat right next to him.

"My name's Dan Caulfield. I'm a former Marine officer, and a huge fan of yours. I have a business I'd like to tell you about," I said. He laughed, pointed to the seat in front of us, and said, "You see that guy, there? He has a gun."

I replied, "I told you, sir, I'm a Marine. I'm not afraid of bullets." A few weeks later, I was pitching the senior leadership of Fed Ex. The good news was that we convinced them to fund a national military recruiting program with Hire Quality. The bad news was that we didn't have the company structure or wherewithal to execute the program.

To make a long story short, we failed with FedEx. We had the perfect solution for the perfect customer, but we weren't able to deliver successfully. We delivered the candidates to the businesses, but the companies weren't hiring the candidates. So we were fired, which was extremely embarrassing. It wasn't until later that I discovered that ex-military personnel are three-to-five times *less* likely to get hired for the same job than their civilian counterparts. Perception became reality.

But none of that mattered. It was my job to make sure FedEx got to play out this enormous opportunity to hire thousands of quality people coming out the military in every major city in America. We failed because I didn't understand how big corporations worked, and I created unrealistic expectations for my clients. I sold potential, and potential was bought. But the reality of the hiring process and the newness of the Internet delivered much more down-to-earth results.

Getting off the Beach

I now understand the things that are important to creating a successful business—mostly because I didn't do them in my first year of business and learned them the hard way. When you're in the military, you hear the saying, "Get off the beach." The saying means someday, as a Marine, you'll be on a landing craft motoring to some beach in some God-forsaken little-known part of the world. The enemy will be waiting there, ready to kill you. At that point, only one thing matters: *Get off the beach.*

With start-ups, it's tough getting off the beach because there are so many enemies and obstacles trying to stop you. At some point, that seminal moment will come when you have to either get off the beach or die trying, just like a Marine. The more knowledge you have, the better your chances. So here are a few thoughts I've gathered through years of experience and years of mistakes that might help.

First, when you're starting a company, identify a clear mission, vision, and set of core values for your business. Who do you want to be, how will you act, how will you communicate with the various stakeholders of your business, and what do you want to look like?

Second, assign clearly defined roles and responsibilities to help you accomplish your task. Then tell everybody how their success will be measured and how they will be held accountable. Now when start-ups hire me as a consultant to organize them and set a strategic plan, what I see over and over again is people who are not focused on the right things and people who are not executing the plan. I always ask business leaders to tell me their three to five top priorities. Then we put the appropriate measurements in place to make sure people are executing those priorities.

Third, stop planning, and go sell something! Go out and get customers. You don't need sales people to sell something. You don't need materials and fancy "leave behinds." You just need a list of targets. Call them, ask questions, and listen. Identify the pain, and the impact of that pain on your potential client personally, professionally, and for the company. Position your solutions so that people can say "Yes." People buy because they trust you. But ask for money up front. The best place for growth capital is from customers. Ask for the money you need to create the solution they require. If they trust you, because you have proven to them you know what they want and can provide it, they will pay you in advance.

Fourth, find the right people to manage the various roles and responsibilities, not just whoever is available. It doesn't have to be someone with 100 separate job skills. It can be someone who's only good at that one thing. I don't even try to improve on people's weaknesses. I couldn't care less about their weaknesses. I'm only interested in their strengths.

Fifth, after you have some traction, meaning you've made some sales to real customers who are actually paying you for what you do, secure the capital you need. I still start and consult for bootstrap companies, because I know I can get a few customers paying me in advance and get some traction for very little capital. All I need is the Internet and a phone.

> *I now understand the things that are important to creating a successful business —mostly because I didn't do them in my first year of business and learned them the hard way.*

TweetPhoto.com is one of the biggest success stories you'll find, and the founders and I chose not to get capital to fund the start-up. We decided the right way to capitalize the company was to get a strategic partner with a leading brand in the online photo-sharing marketplace. We literally had three potential targets, and the one we wanted was Kodak. We got them.

The reason you need capital in business is not for shiny brochures. You need capital to attract and retain the best people in the world. Recruiting the best people you can find early on in business was something I didn't do. Instead, I hired the people I could afford. It just happened that one of them was my college roommate. He ended up being my COO, and a huge asset for me. I got lucky—that time.

Sixth, manage your cash. It's a really simple idea. I don't have an MBA, and I don't want to get an MBA—but I do have a Ph.D. in cash flow. I'm the king of cash flow. I always ask for money up front and, as amazing as that is for many people, it's usually what I get. I also pay vendors late. It's not a point of pride. I'm just not paying you until I get paid. It may sound like I'm taking advantage of vendors, but I set expectations so that it's never an issue.

My final words of wisdom go back to the main reason Hire Quality is (unfortunately) not a $100 million company today. In the end, I sold Hire Quality to Ross Perot on December 31, 1999. When people hear that. they think it was a huge success. I actually started a new business with Mr. Perot and learned much from him, but in the end, it was a financial disaster. I literally had to start all over. The depression and self-doubt I accumulated through the process took years to heal. I made the sale. But it didn't play out as I'd dreamed it would on that Friday morning when I was standing on a Chicago Street in my skivvies.

I had the perfect client and lost them because I over-promised and under-delivered. I had the perfect buyer and partner to grow a truly big business, but again, I set my expectations so high that I couldn't hope to reach them. I didn't hire the best people, and I didn't hold them accountable to a short list of priorities and defined metrics. I may have failed, but I didn't fail to learn the lessons from my failure. I just wish I could have learned them without the pain. If I only knew then what I know now.

In the end, business isn't really rocket science. It comes down to five simple concepts. Did I mention that Marines like to keep things simple?
1. Build the strategic plan.
2. Define the roles, responsibilities, and metrics to measure success.
3. Sell something to someone.
4. Hire the best people for the roles you establish.
5. Get the capital you need to do more of number three and number four!

 Dan is a senior executive and has helped six companies navigate hyper-growth and the angel/venture funding process. Dan has helped the companies he has served raise a total of $30 million. In most cases, Dan has taken a key executive role leading up to the VC investment. Most recently, Dan was the CEO of TweetPhoto.com, a photo-sharing service that is globally ranked in the top 300 Websites by Alexa.com. Prior to joining TweetPhoto, Dan was a board member and Chief Operating Officer at Mojopages.com, board member and Acting Chief Marketing Officer at Dayak.com, Senior Manager at Cap Gemini Ernst & Young, President of MilitaryHub.com, and the Founder & President of Hire Quality, Inc. Dan is also the Founder and Chairman of the Board of the Armed Forces Support Foundation, which operates HireaHero.org. He also co-founded another not-for-profit called Helmets to Hardhats. HAH and H2H are nationally recognized as the models for public-private military transition programs. Dan is a United States Marine Corps veteran.

Being Homeless
Is a Good Motivator

17

Core Legal Translations
Blake Canedy

This is a story from a masterful entrepreneur. I selected this story because Blake's life is more than just a rags-to-riches fairytale. His is a story of discovering the importance of living in the moment. Blake has profited from more opportunities in one lifetime than most of us have had the awareness to see, let alone act upon. And all through his challenges, his companies, and his successes, he's humbly played to his strength within the moment...he's been true to the present.

—Ken

Thirty years ago, at the age of twenty, I was homeless. When my friends learn about my past, most have a hard time believing it's true. But it is true. I was homeless for two years.

Living in a van and being hungry were tough teachers. There was little room for error, and the downside to making an error was potentially horrific. That horror constantly stared me in the face. Simply learning to be present in and constantly paying attention to the truth of the moment led me out of homelessness and toward entrepreneurship.

From the time that I was in fourth grade, I knew I wanted to be an entrepreneur. While other kids wanted to be athletes, fighter pilots, or movie stars, I thought that being an entrepreneur would be the most exciting path I could possibly take. Even the title "entrepreneur" had a spiritual sort of meaning to me. At that young age, I knew that to be a complete person, I needed to be an entrepreneur. I imagined people introducing me at parties: "This is Blake Canedy. He's an entrepreneur." Nothing sounded better to me. It didn't matter what business I'd start; I just wanted to start one. Everything about the concept of entrepreneurship appealed to me, from the responsibilities to the perks.

As a young boy, I had a recurring dream that filled me with awe and happiness: Walking across a factory floor toward my office and having employees say hello to me, smile, and ask me questions as I walked. For me, being an entrepreneur wasn't a passing fad. It was a lifelong dream. I just never imagined how difficult it would be to learn the lessons I needed to be successful.

I grew up in Europe and Asia. I didn't know much about my biological father other than the fact that he was a pilot in the American Air Force. My stepdad, who was also an American Air Force officer, raised me. Unfortunately, we had what could be called a distant relationship.

My mother was a proud woman who was born and raised in England. She loved her new husband, and very soon, they had two children together. Depending upon the country in which we were stationed, we alternated between living on the military base and living off-base in the local communities.

Given lots of freedom to explore the American Air Force bases and the local communities, I became pretty good at meeting people and making friends. Unlike typical American schools, those I attended on the military bases were more like small, private schools. Socially, I had an absolute blast, especially in high school.

I graduated from Lakenheath High School in England. When it came time to pick a college, I looked at maps of the United States and decided upon the University of Missouri, Columbia, mostly because it was located in the middle. I'd always struggled academically. Today, kids dealing with problems like I had are diagnosed with Attention Deficit Disorder, but back then I was just considered a struggling student with poor grades.

Predictably, I did poorly in college. After three semesters, I didn't make the required GPA to stay in school. I was confused and even embarrassed about doing so poorly. My confidence was seriously shaken. I wasn't in a good place emotionally or mentally. I called my parents who said something to the effect of good luck, and then they cut me off financially. The only money I had was in my pocket. I was shaken, homeless, alone, and broke in a country that I still didn't completely understand.

For a short time, I got caught up with "what ifs": What if I get sick? What if I can't figure things out? What if something happens to me? Would anybody even know? I soon realized my truth in that moment was to focus on the more basic things: Where am I going to sleep? What am I going to eat? What can I do to make money—and fast?

I vividly remember standing in front of campus housing and thinking, "I'm starting from right here in this very spot. This is my beginning. There is nothing else but right now. The past doesn't matter, and I can't do anything about the future. I only have right now." For maybe the first time in my life, I began to realize the power in "right now." Developing a sense of right now—to stay present in the moment, make the best decision I can in that moment, and start walking toward what I want—was one of the best business and life lessons I've ever learned.

I soon decided that I wanted to be near the ocean and that California would offer a more pleasing climate to be homeless in than the freezing winters of Missouri. How to get there was the next question. With an $800 paycheck from a medical research project I had participated in, I bought a $750 VW van and found three people who wanted a ride to California. The deal was that they bought the fast food, gas, and the oil (and the van burned lots of oil). After buying a few supplies and maps, I was on my way to California with three paying customers, a piece-of-crap van, and eight dollars total to my name. I was exhilarated because in that moment I wasn't hungry, and I was moving towards my goal and had a "home"—even if that home burned lots of oil.

I found what most people would call a menial job working on fruit orchards. I called it an opportunity. And in the evenings and weekends, I taught scuba diving to groups of students and eventually became fast friends with my co-instructor. We each had an interest in business and spent many hours discussing entrepreneurial ventures. My entrepreneurial juices were reawakened.

Eventually, I moved from the van to the cheapest hotel I could find, which was also the only hotel I could afford. It was cheap for a reason. It was in the worst part of town, and prostitutes frequently used it by the hour. I was constantly on guard for trouble. I was tired of living that way, and knew that I had to find a way out. But my resume was basically nonexistent—no college degree, no real work experience.

By looking at my current situation and my resume, very few people would've bet on me making much of myself. I realized in that moment that I had to take action to improve my situation. I needed skills.

I got a job selling vacuum cleaners. It was certainly not glamorous, but it offered something I badly needed—money. But more importantly, the job taught me how to sell. The company I worked for had its sales system down to a science. After two weeks of classroom work, including lots of role-playing, I hit the streets. I sold vacuum cleaners door-to-door for a year. By the time I left, my closing ratio was the highest in the company's history. For every two appointments, I closed one of them. It wasn't much money, but I'd learned how to sell.

Good things started happening. I went from living in the cheapest and scariest hotels in the city to finding a room to rent from a nice family in a nice neighborhood. For the first time in two years, I actually felt safe going to sleep at night. I began to dream again. And I began aching to figure out a way to become an entrepreneur.

An Open Window

My first business came about because I overheard a conversation at a party. My friend mentioned that he'd paid all his own college and living expenses by operating his own business. I quickly cornered him to ask what this business was. He told me it was a commercial window cleaning service.

The very next Saturday, I met him at his apartment, and after we talked, he grabbed his window washing gear and we stopped at the very first commercial business we came across. It was a busy deli. My friend asked the owner if we could wash his windows half a dozen times because he was training me. The owner said no problem. My friend then asked the owner if he would pay us with two lunches, and he agreed.

After twenty minutes of washing the same windows over and over, we ordered our lunch. That may have been the best tasting sandwich I'd ever eaten. I knew that I'd found my first business, and I felt free because I was stepping onto my path to entrepreneurship.

I asked my friend a million questions about the window cleaning business. After asking all my business questions, there was one non-business question that just kept nagging me, and I had to ask: *If he could make more money in less time being in business, any business, why in the world would he choose working a job?* His answer amazed me. He just didn't care for uncertainty or risk. He was happier having a job. He liked receiving a paycheck. I realized I had more to learn. I needed to learn how to create a work environment that offered fulfillment and security.

I immediately ordered a thousand business cards. As soon as the cards were ready, I took a day off from work. I put a handful of business cards into my pocket and drove to an area near where I lived that had lots of commercial businesses. I gathered up my courage, and I walked into the first business on the street. With a very simple pitch, but one that I had practiced for about a week in front of my bathroom mirror, I asked the owner for his business. Not only did I get the business, but on that one street, on that first day, I landed enough window cleaning business to equal about 25 percent of my paycheck from my current job.

My first entrepreneurial venture was immediately profitable, and those profits came in quick cash. It allowed me to pay for an apartment, pay my bills, and buy a small truck. I now had the time and the stability to enroll in community college and give academics another try. I wanted to learn more about business. What motivated and interested me most was the thought of starting a second, more lucrative business.

> *At that young age, I knew that to be a complete person, I needed to be an entrepreneur.*
>
> *I imagined people introducing me at parties: "This is Blake Canedy. He's an entrepreneur."*

It occurred to me that the best way to learn about the real world of business was to ask relevant questions of people who were in business. Conveniently, those exact people were my customers. It was another example of the power of right now. I started asking questions about how they started their companies, how they raised the money, their backgrounds and business experience, what sort of skills they had to learn, how they planned to grow the business, and what they wanted to achieve.

I had just over a hundred customers, and I walked in and chatted with hundreds of other business owners. I talked to everyone from the deli owners to the people in professional office buildings. I think many of them were amused by the window washer asking them about their businesses. But most opened up and talked with me.

I began to notice patterns, and by pure accident, I started to predict which companies would succeed or fail. At first, my predictions came from just my own ideas about how I didn't see such and such business lasting more than X number of months. In time, I realized that my predictions were accurate. I began to take my analysis and predictions more seriously. I noticed a few commonalities about the businesses that failed.

First, their failure had very little to do with their service or the product they offered; it had more to do with the people who were running the show, and more specifically, with how much homework and how many questions those people asked about their businesses.

Second was the attitude I noticed in the businesses. The companies that treated their staff and their vendors poorly also seemed to treat their customers poorly, and it was almost always a straight line to business failure.

I started to feel pretty smart. I was a window washer, arguably a business that didn't stretch me to my full capabilities, but I was able to accurately predict which companies would thrive and which ones would fail. After talking to hundreds of business owners, I saw a pattern for business success: Formulate every question possible, be open to hear the answers, take everything learned and write a business plan that includes financial projections, and treat everyone—the customers, the staff, and the vendors—with respect.

After a few years, I sold the commercial window cleaning business. I was offered a decent price to sell. I'd saved some money, learned a lot, and now it was time to stretch. I knew almost immediately that my buyer would fail. Analyzing businesspeople was now something that came automatically, and I couldn't shut it off. It was a simple analysis; my buyer simply didn't ask me enough questions. I badly wanted to tell him more about the details of the business, but he acted like he knew all the answers. A few months after I sold my business, my customers began calling and telling me that new owner was terrible, wasn't regular, and had finally stopped showing up altogether.

I felt smart. I supposed that not just anybody could run a window cleaning service. Next, I saw the boom in car phones, and I wanted in on it. By utilizing everything I'd learned, I started a mobile car phone business. That business did very well, and my financial position improved. But I wasn't thrilled with the direction of the industry. I could see that the independent dealer was going to be replaced by the carriers. I suppose I could have viewed this as horrible news, but I didn't. I stayed present in the moment and just considered it information. I learned that what may be considered bad news is actually good news if it's discovered early enough for you to act on it.

I started looking around for another opportunity, a better opportunity, something that I could leverage. I opened my next business using my same formula: asking lots of questions, writing a plan with financials, talking to everyone, and being respectful to everyone. This business was a court reporting firm, and I went into that business for the perfect reason—to make money.

I was twenty-nine years old. My plan was to quickly build the company and hire staff who wanted and valued their jobs and who could consistently do the daily work better than I would. In the beginning, the business was run by just my wife and me. I was involved up to my eyeballs in every aspect of the business. I often worked all day and all night. I remember many nights looking up at my wall clock and seeing that it was 4 a.m. What kept me going were my goals and my written plan. I soon grew the business, and even better than that, it became extremely profitable.

Within four years, I was able to buy the big house on the hill with the spectacular view, and I did so without having to sell my townhouse to raise the down payment. It felt good. I started to collect oil paintings, and I paired that interest with short trips to cities that had nice art districts. I had the sports cars, the great clothes, the watches, and I took lavish vacations. The president of my bank knew who I was and offered me tickets to events—expensive tickets. I had what was called a "private banker." My financial life was nice. I spent lots of money, but I also saved lots of money. I completely and totally fell in love with the right girl. My marriage was fantastic, and we started having babies. I felt awesome, and I felt free. I was building my own family. I was dedicated to being the best husband and the best father I could be.

It wasn't very often that it came up in conversation, but on the occasions when I told people that I'd been homeless, most thought I was kidding. Mostly because my 'right now' was so far removed from my past. I used to have fun saying that I loved business because I could hire people to do my work, and then I could hire more people, salespeople, to get me more work. I hired very well, and I was able to spend less and less time in my office, spending more and more time with my wife and family. All those years of asking questions and seeing the patterns in businesses were paying dividends.

I ran my court reporting firm for almost two decades, and then I read an article in a psychology magazine. The article alluded to the fact that to really have an exciting life, you needed to quit while you're at the top of your career and challenge yourself to do something completely different. So I did. I sold the company to a perfect buyer out of New York, a very smart CEO who I knew would be successful.

After taking a little time off, I knew I still had the calling to be an entrepreneur. I decided to jump into the globalization trend. I followed all my steps, and after asking lots of questions and doing considerable research, I wrote a business plan with financials and started a new business, this time a language interpreting and translation company.

As I write this, right now, in this moment, I'm genuinely happy to be able to continue following my dream. Will this dream be my last one? Or will another opportunity present itself to me down the road? It's hard to say, but one thing is for sure: Being in the moment and moving forward not from the past but from the present have served me well. I think I'll stick with it.

Blake Canedy is founder and president of Core Legal Translations, a language company providing expert professional translation and interpretation services for the legal industry. Previously, Blake started and ran several businesses including a window washing service, a cell phone sales company, and a court reporting firm. He has a lifetime interest in martial arts and holds an advanced black belt in traditional karate. He enjoys blacksmithing, scuba diving, and hiking, and holds a master's degree in spiritual psychology.

Uncertainty Can Be Empowering

18

Hire Better
Jonathan Davis

Entrepreneurs are ambitious and competitive, wildly so. I probably don't have to tell you that. I think it's a sickness, and we all have it. Jonathan's story struck me because it's the one that shows just how much we wrap our identities up in our businesses and how much pressure we put on ourselves to succeed. This isn't a problem when things are flying high, but it can be devastating when things aren't going well. Jonathan takes you on a first-year journey from the ultra highs to the rock-bottom lows of his business. Through it all, he teaches us some valuable business lessons while showing us that being mindful of how far we've come is just as important as keeping our eyes on the prize.

—Ken

It was five days before Thanksgiving 2008 when I told a guy I'd known for ten years, "I've got to let you go, and your severance package is your laptop." It was a nice laptop, but not *that* nice.

Unfortunately, by then, the economy had tanked. My fast-growing human resources consulting business was in a free-fall and nearing failure. You've probably seen footage of the Hindenburg blimp. That was us—a giant fireball crashing to earth in what seemed like a minute of elapsed time.

Just six weeks before Thanksgiving, business was down 62 percent. In November, it was down 84 percent. The velocity of the free fall was stunning—it happened almost overnight. We went from twenty-two employees to just two part-time people and me sitting around an office eyeing each other like death-row inmates on execution day.

I wasn't sleeping. I had hemorrhoids. I had ulcers. I was vomiting daily. There were days when I just didn't want to get out of bed. I felt so depressed and overwhelmed that I was in complete shock.

I really thought I was done for.

Which Way Do We Go?

So, now that I've scared the hell out of you and made you wonder why you ever chose to be an entrepreneur, let me give you some perspective on this venture— and some good news, too.

How many times have people who aren't entrepreneurs said to you, "Wow, I'm so impressed with how you deal with risk"? That's not really accurate.

What an entrepreneur is really good at is dealing with uncertainty because it's a constant part of your life, like that annoying mole you never had removed. Every hour of every day as an entrepreneur, you make decisions without knowing whether they're the right decisions.

You can't predict the economy, you can't predict if your business partner is going to screw you, and you can't predict a long list of other variables. So you never truly know if you're on the right path.

Some people will tell you they knew all along their idea would succeed—that they knew the direction from the start. Economists will tell you they knew all along that the economy was going into the tank, but it's all complete crap. What economists are really good at is hindsight—explaining the economy six months after the new reality has arrived.

There is no handbook for most of the decisions entrepreneurs make; no clear-cut choice that screams, "Go this way!"

It's like being a new parent. Nobody tells you what to do at two in the morning when you're holding your four-month-old and she has a 104-degree fever. You just sit there, scared to death. You can use all the information and people at your disposal to make an informed decision—a logical decision—but in the end *you* have to make the choice. You have to provide the care.

The great thing about all that uncertainty is that it's empowering. You learn to make decisions even when your hands are shaking, when people close to you say, "No way," or even when a part of you says, "Am I sure?"

When you think about it, what's the alternative to making that decision? More research? More development? More time dragging your feet? At some point, you have to take the leap. At some point, you need to have faith that you've dotted all the "I"s and crossed all the "T"s.

When I think back on the empowering things in my life, the choice I made in January of 2008 to rely on myself and grow my own business was easily the best decision I've ever made, even though eleven months later things looked pretty grim. Up until that point, I hadn't had the courage to do something for myself—to step out without somebody else as a partner or with somebody else's money.

It took the last in a sequence of events to finally push me to that brink.

Taking the Leap

In late May 2006, I got involved with a start-up insurance company, and by the summer we'd raised $100 million to get it going. I was running around the country, visiting all these great cities, meeting all these interesting people, raising lots of money, and thinking, "This is cool. I'm an entrepreneur."

It satisfied an urge in me. I felt energized. I was happy.

Well, it didn't take long for me to realize that by raising all that money for someone else, I was essentially an employee for a board—not an entrepreneur. And boards are tough bosses because they rarely ever give you positive feedback. They only come in every nine or ten weeks to beat the crap out of you for eight hours, and then they leave. So you're performing with all the uncertainty of an entrepreneur but with a really heavy-handed whip on you and people who are always second-guessing your decisions looking over your shoulder. By the summer of 2007, I started thinking, "It would be nice just to be my own boss."

So I turned my attention back toward a small consulting company I'd started in December of 2004. I hadn't been giving it any attention, but it just kept going. It was like the little engine that could, and the time just felt right.

By January of 2008, I'd satisfied all my obligations to the board of the insurance company, and I said, "Guys, I'm out."

It was scary to jump off that ledge. I had no idea where or how I would land. But that first year in business was a defining moment for me because it was my choice. I was living on my terms.

Riding the Wave

It's been said that a rising tide raises all ships, and let me tell you, all ships were up in the spring of 2008. The economy was going like gangbusters, and so was my business. We were just a few months old, and we couldn't control the growth. By that summer, the business was growing 15 to 20 percent a week, and we were taking on clients without even knowing how we would service them. I didn't have the people, I didn't have the resources, and I had no real game plan.

I hired a vice president of operations who had no experience in operations. When the opportunity came to triple in size, we said, "Why not? Let's do it." We even had what we referred to as "revenue fairies." Every time we had a day when we were almost caught up, they knocked on the door and delivered us a new client.

> **When you think about it, what's the alternative to making that decision?**
>
> **More research? More development? More time dragging your feet?**
>
> **At some point, you have to take the leap.**

We didn't know how or why we were so good—we just reveled in it. What we learned later is that winning is the best deodorant because it masks the stench of all your problems. We didn't know where the rotting carcasses of our business were because we hadn't taken the time to look for them. We didn't need to. We were growing fast, and we had this dangerous sense of security—a sense that we could do no wrong.

Guess what? We were wrong.

The Fall

I remember sitting at dinner in late 2008, just before Christmas, looking at my two young kids, my wife, and my parents, and thinking, "What am I going to do now?" There was really nothing left to salvage of my business. At least, it felt that way. In the course of a year, I'd shot to the moon and came crashing down again at breakneck speed.

I'd gone from this fast-growing company to fighting for eight billable hours so that I could make my mortgage payment. In truth, I was still making enough to pay my bills, but my wife and I had curtail our lifestyle dramatically. There were no vacations, no date nights, and we went from shopping at the high-end grocery store to bargain hunting at the discount store.

It was so emotionally draining that it numbed me—I felt like I was sleepwalking through life. I knew I was a lousy employee, so going to work for anyone else would be a really bad idea, but by now, I had this steaming bag of dog feces as a business, and nobody seemed to want to buy anything we had to sell.

With no other choice, I poured myself back into the business and learned some important things in the process. It was another defining moment in my life—a lousy one, but an educational and important one.

Lessons Learned

There's a saying that advice is just someone else's bad experience with all the dirt wiped off. It's certainly true for me. My experiences taught me some valuable lessons that I think apply broadly.

Lesson #1:
If you're making cuts, don't take the death-by-a-thousand cuts approach.

One of the things I did right was to immediately make massive cuts to my staff. My worry at the beginning was, "If I let them go now, I'll never get them back." Wrong.

If you're losing money on a service business there's something terribly wrong because there are no costs other than your people. If there's no work, why do you have them?

Lesson #2:

Don't throw money at the problem.

I didn't dive into my business line of credit to bail water out of a sinking ship when I had no clear sense of when or how I was going to pay it back. I know a lot of people who used their lines of credit, and their debt became unmanageable.

Lesson #3:

Do what you've got to do.

Like I said before, my wife and I cut our lifestyle way back. We eliminated as much of the superfluous stuff as we could. We did it because we had to, and that same idea applies to clients. When we were struggling to stay alive, we took on some clients who weren't a good fit for our business. They didn't play to our strengths. I regret it now, because a lot of those clients drove me crazy, but I felt that if someone needed my services, and they were going to pay me money, I had no choice. I was in survival mode.

Lesson #4:

Find a mentor—or better yet, find a bunch of them.

Lois Melbourne, who's the CEO of Aquire in Dallas and a mentor of mine, told me, "If it's lonely at the top, you're doing it wrong." Her point is this: Somebody's been through your situation before. Find out how to tap into and use that person's knowledge.

Entrepreneurs' Organization has been crucial in every decision I've made about the way I now do business. When you're a new member of EO, you're trained on how to share experiences with other members rather than give advice. When you talk to advisors and mentors, don't accept their advice passively. Ask them about the experiences that created those opinions. What successes and failures led them to offer that advice? You can derive a lot more from experiences than you can from advice.

The final thing I would mention is this: When my company was growing quickly, I never took the time to truly examine how we could have done things better. I'm not talking about minor tweaks. I'm talking about re-examining the foundations of the business.

Back in March 2009, I was still down in the depths, just limping along. A friend of mine was in town, and I asked her to take a look at the business and strip it down to the studs. It was great to have that extra set of eyes pouring over my business. It helped me look inward, and it helped me see things I'd been overlooking. Her perspective gave me new direction, new insights, and renewed passion. I was able to re-engage our software development team, and we rewrote our proprietary software and focused on the next stage of our business. We re-evaluated from the ground up our internal process, and the way we did things. And I started reading about ways to integrate other ideas into our business.

With this newfound sense of purpose, I went to my wife and said, "Honey, I need your permission to leverage everything the family's got to see if we can pull out of this." To her credit—and my amazement—she supported me. But she had some conditions.

Behind every great entrepreneur is somebody with a brain, and she was my brain, my sense of reason. She helped me realize that if I was going to try this, I'd better believe in it, commit to it fully, and, of course, show her a return on the investment. "We're not going to do this just because you're bored," she said.

Out of the Darkness

Today, we have thirty employees, and we're bigger than we've ever been revenue-wise, client-wise, and in geographic reach. It doesn't mean we won't have bad days down the road. We have, and we will. But we're stronger and wiser.

For my first two years in EO, I was always embarrassed to go to events because I felt like people would look at me and say, "He's not a real entrepreneur. He's just faking it." I struggled because it seemed to me everyone else had businesses that were more successful than mine.

I have a tendency to focus on the summit, to look only at the top of the mountain, and to think that's the only place worth being and that I'll never reach it. But here's the truth: There will always be a person with more clients and more revenue than you.

It's taken me being down in a hole and digging out to understand how life and business really are all about the journey. Your journey *is* the destination. That's why, in the first twenty minutes of every company meeting we have at Hire Better, I now take time to look back down the mountain to see how far we've come. We share stories, talk about little victories, and celebrate accomplishments. If you don't look back on all those miles you've covered and every step you've taken, you'll never be satisfied.

When I look back on our crash in the fall of 2008—our Hindenburg—I realize now that it taught me some vital lessons. I hope I don't have to crash and burn like that ever again, but at least I'll have a better idea of how to survive it if I do—and I'll know what smoke smells like.

 Jonathan Davis is Co-Founder and CEO of Hire Better and has spent the last decade helping build companies from scratch. After five years as a principal of a staff-leasing and HR-outsourcing firm, Jonathan started working on the one area in which he saw the biggest lack of viable solutions for growing companies: talent acquisition. Today, he is responsible for the strategic leadership of Hire Better Solutions as it continues to revolutionize the world of recruiting by focusing on metrics and innovation. Jonathan is a member of the Young Entrepreneurs' Organization, is the Austin Champion for the EO Accelerator Program, and sits on the EO Global Committee for Emerging Programs.

Remind Me...Why Did We Get into Business?

19

Speaker, Author, and Entrepreneur
Troy Hazard

Troy is a serial entrepreneur, and in the pages that follow, he re-counts exactly what led up to starting his first venture and the five lessons he learned during his first year. You might say he took a leap of faith, and like many entrepreneurs, he had a realization during his first twelve months on his own. Call it an "Oh crap, moment" that both scared him and got him moving in the right direction. We've all been there. Troy's probably been there many times since, in one way or another. Troy talks about passion and he rains it on everyone he meets.

—Ken

So remind me—why did I get into business? It was late 1989, and I was driving in to work at the radio station for another early start to the day.

The days were starting to feel like the movie *Groundhog Day*, in which Bill Murray keeps reliving the exact same twenty-four hours over and over again. Start the day at 5 a.m. Produce the breakfast show. When the djs came off air at 9 a.m., produce and pre-record their comedy segments for the next day's show until about 11 a.m. Go to station meetings until mid-afternoon. Inhale some food at my mixing console in my studio. Throw more coffee down my throat in preparation for the second half of the day. Stay locked in the darkness of the studio for another ten hours before driving home sometime around 10 p.m., only to swill two or three beers on the couch and pass out. Wake up and be ready to do it all again.

This had been my life for three months. As I drove to the studio that morning in the darkness and the silence, only one thought slipped out of my mouth into the morning air: "This isn't fun anymore."

Radio had been a great part of my life for many years. I loved my time on the air, and I loved my time as program and production manager, but it was beginning to be something other than what I'd signed up for. The station had been through multiple ownership changes in two years, and the most recent one was the toughest. For some reason, my new manager just kept pushing the envelope, loading me up with enough work for three people, and giving me unachievable challenges everyday—seemingly just for his own entertainment.

That morning as the breakfast team came off the air and I had my first break for the day, I walked into my boss' office at 9 a.m. and simply said, "I'm done! You've pushed me too far, and for no reason. Clearly you have someone else you have in mind for the job. You should let them have it."

And just like that, my radio career came to an end—and I was unemployed.

I got home early that night, sat in the dark, and thought to myself, "Hmmm, what have I done?"

I rang one of my business mentors, a real-estate guru named Graham Hogg, and asked his advice. We decided to put my apartment on the market because real estate was booming at the time and the inevitable crash was coming soon. It was time to cash in on the ride. So I did, and we sold it the next day.

I rang my mother next and said, "I just sold my apartment... oh, yeah, and I quit my job on Friday." There was a pause, and then the inevitable question, "So, what are you going to do now?"

My very confident, yet shallow, response was, "I think I'll go buy a crappy house and renovate it. You know, see if I can cash in on the real-estate boom for a little while and make some money. Want to chip in? We'll do it together?"

And just like that, I was in business. My mom and I each threw $30,000 into an account, registered a business name, and then as if it was our destiny, we were in the renovation business with our new company. We named it New Address.

A few weeks later, we bought a filthy three-bedroom home in an outer city suburb. The walls looked like the previous owners had a budding graffiti artist in the family; the carpet had morphed from carpet with a bit of dog hair in it to dog hair with a hint of carpet color; the backyard looked like it would make a great location for an episode of "Survivor"; and the kitchen looked like something from a 1960s cereal commercial, only you'd never dream of ever eating anything there. The house was perfect!

My mother, Bev, did all of the interior decorating and design, and I did the deals with the real estate agents, carpenters, landscape guys, flooring guys, and any other vendors. And away we went. I guess I didn't have time to wonder if I'd made the right decision or not because one house led to two, and two led to three, and three to four, and you get the picture. We fixed them and flipped them as quickly as we could. Sometimes we got in and out of the property in just three weeks!

The market was hot, and so were we. On one occasion alone, I can recall settling on a property and saying to the agent, "Call me in four weeks, we'll be done here."

After the fifth week he pounded on the front door saying, "You've listed the property with someone else?"

"For sure," I said, "I told you to ring me in four weeks, and you didn't."

"I didn't believe you that you'd be done by then," he said.

I just smiled and said, "Then maybe you better start listening to your clients" as I shut the door.

I was having a blast. I'd get up at dawn, paint until mid-morning, do some deals with vendors and agents until about lunchtime, set everyone up on site for the afternoon, and then head off to lunch with my mates. I'd get home sometime later that afternoon and continue painting into the night while drinking a few beers and running the stereo full tilt. It was the perfect job, right up until I realized it wasn't a job—it was a business.

I was walking down the beach with a mate of mine, telling him about the events of the last six months in my new-found career, giving him the highlights:
- We'd traded half a dozen properties.
- Five more properties were under contract or about to settle.
- We'd made about a 20 percent margin on each of the properties.

- And we were about $500,000 in debt. Okay, so that fact got my *own* attention.

As the words came out of my mouth, I went a little quiet. For my friend, this was no surprise—he was used to doing million-dollar deals every other day. For me, this was all new. Until I quit my job, I'd only had a $45,000 mortgage and a busted MG convertible that was more of a pushcart than a sports car.

I was silent as we walked. I could feel my pulse quicken a little and my brain start to buzz a bit. Clearly, I needed to develop a better strategy for the business, or it would all fall down like the proverbial house of cards.

I must have gone a little pale because my mate quietly asked me, "You all right?" To which I responded in my best strategic fashion, "Let's find a bar!"

The next few hours were good for me. I'd reached a turning point in business. That day, I walked onto the beach just having fun as a self-employed bloke. I walked off the beach as a small-businessperson about to learn some early lessons. I spent the next few days with my friend, and I grilled him on how he ran his business, how he planned, and how he put money together so that it went in and out as it should without leaving the cupboard bare. It was fascinating, and oh, so frightening!

To me, this conversation and this learning were significant. It was my very first realization that I now had way more responsibility than I did as a manager and employee, even though I'd run teams of up to fifteen people and budgets well in excess of the property value I was trading. This was now totally my responsibility, and it was me, and me alone, who I could applaud for my win or blame for my loss!

During the next few weeks, I jammed as much information into my head as I could. I read books, talked to people, and went to seminars, all in an effort to try and work out what I *should* be doing and what I was currently doing wrong, or, through sheer luck, doing right.

Then I set about writing up a very basic business plan and did some forensic accounting on each of the properties we were trading. From this, I learned some very simple lessons, which helped me through the next nine companies I would own.

Show Me the Money!

It became painfully obvious that we were not making money on the *sale* of our properties. Rather, we were making money on the *purchase* of our properties. No matter which way I looked at it, success was always about how well we *bought* houses, not about how well we *sold* them.

The reason for this was that we had more control over the purchase than we did the sale. On the way in, we could source the product ourselves and simply use the realtor as the go-between. On the sale of the property, we had to rely more on the realtor's ability to get the buyer to the table to at least talk.

Lesson #1:
You make money on the buy—not the sell.

I believe that with any product or service, there is no such thing as a "buyer's market" or a "seller's market." It's more about the ability of buyer to buy well from an inexperienced seller who has less confidence in his or her product than the buyer does in his or her negotiating ability.

> *It became painfully obvious that we were not making money on the sale of our properties.*
>
> *Rather, we were making money on the* **purchase** *of our properties.*

To that end, I needed to find more owners in distress and use that to my advantage. It's harsh, I know, but I figured if I didn't push their buttons, then the banks were sure going to. Better to have the money in my bank account than theirs, I reasoned.

Lesson #2:
Smaller sales cycles = bigger profits.

My second "ah-ha" was that we made the most money relative to our speed to market. This was for a number of reasons. There was less marketing cost because the sale time was shorter. There was less holding cost on the cost of money. And there was less time wasted with realtors doing the negotiation tap dance as they continued to treat me like an inexperienced seller and kept trying to get a lower sale price.

These two simple lessons alone improved both our cash flow and our bottom line. Interestingly, I've applied them to every business I've been in since. Regardless of business category, the product, or the service we were selling, without fail, they continue to prove a solid basis for the profitability of a business.

People Power

My next big "ah-ha" was that if I didn't start to surround myself with good people, I was screwed! I couldn't do this on my own, and the people I had working with me, outside of my mother, of course, were all average, at best.

I figured that if I was to get the properties back on the market faster, then I needed to get the best vendors on board to do the renovations as fast as they could to turn the houses around.

Lesson #3:
Be slow to hire, and quick to fire.

In the early days, we were getting vendors mainly as they were available, and cheap would always win. It was all about the best quote. It never struck me that maybe they were available *because* they were cheap. In other words, nobody hired them because they sucked! Even their knuckle-dragging, monosyllabic, and somewhat Chewbacca-like demeanor didn't tip me off. But hey, I was new at this stuff!

For a while, we'd put up with their poor work and poor behavior. Mainly, I was afraid I would find myself in a witness protection program if I fired any of them. But then one day, I figured I needed to start being more diligent in interviewing our potential vendors to see if they were a fit with our business model. We weren't asking for much. We just wanted people to be *good* and *fast*. So after telling all of our existing vendors that I was moving to Mongolia, we changed suburbs *and* vendors.

Lesson #4:
Lead me, feed me, love me, keep me.

With our new-found employment strategy, we began interviewing much better, and we found some stellar vendors to help with the core functions of renovating kitchens, bathrooms, flooring, landscapes, and electrical. The next job was to incentivize them to always do a *good* job *fast*. This meant I needed to lead them more on site and drive them to be the best they could be every day they were on the job.

I did incentive deals with all of them to give them the most reason to work hard, do good work, and deliver early. I asked each of them on each project to give me a timeline to completion. We'd sign off on a letter of agreement on the delivery of that promise. If they beat their delivery timeline, they got a 10 percent bonus. For every day late, I'd take a week longer to pay them. It worked like magic. Together they completed thirteen properties in eighteen months, and only one vendor missed his deadline!

I Can See Clearly Now!

As I came to the end of my first twelve months in business, I can recall once again sitting on a beach staring out to sea, with my feet in the sand and a cold beer in my hand. I started to scribble some notes on a piece of paper folded into three columns, which I'd labeled "The Good," "The Bad," and "The Ugly."

For sure, the *good* part of the year for me was that I was out and working on my own. There were no more management changes, useless meetings, idiot bosses, and eighteen-hour days for four hours pay.

The *bad* were the moments throughout the year when I realized I'd lost touch with the money in and the money out. And I promised myself not to be in that position again. Over the years, no matter which company I've owned or how busy I am, I've always been acutely aware of what is, and is not, in the bank at any one point in time. It's one of my few talents, and it has kept me out of bankruptcy on more than one occasion.

The *ugly* were the times when we were actually living in some of the properties we were renovating, mainly to save money and to be able to work the hours we wanted. This was ugly because it was hard on me and on my then-wife. I made a note to myself to keep an eye on balance. This is something I have struggled with for much of my working career. Thankfully, now after twenty years in business, I feel I've finally mastered it.

That night, as the sun began to set and the waves slipped further out on the sand with the tide, I wrote myself one last lesson for the year...

Lesson #5:
Without vision, I have no idea where I'm going.

I'd started my first year with no idea where I was going, except, perhaps, that I wanted to finish the year and be clear. I knew I needed to be clear on what I wanted to achieve in year two.

For sure, my first year in business was a ride. And the last nineteen years have been an adventure. As I reflect at the half-time siren of my life, I'm looking forward to not running back onto the field as the quarterback in the second half, but rather to sitting on the bench working on strategy and enjoying the game—there's less chance of injury.

Troy Hazard
Speaker • Author • Entrepreneur

 Troy Hazard founded and nurtured ten businesses over two decades and experienced the gamut from massive financial loss to stunning success. He is a business consultant, international speaker, author of *The Naked Entrepreneur*, and past Global President of Entrepreneurs' Organization. He's a regular guest business commentator on Fox Business, the Biz Radio Network, and the Business Talk Radio Network, and he hosts the successful national network television shows "Inside Franchising" and "Don't Come Monday." Troy's "Lessons from the Edge" provide businesses with potent tools tested in real-world situations, not learned in business school.

Higher Purpose

20

Parker Finch Management
James Small

Challenges are as much a part of business as they are a part of life. But what happens when business and personal challenges converge and hit you like the perfect storm? In this story, Jim proves that entrepreneurs use their innate strengths of passion, dedication, and work ethics to beat whatever hits them. They see hardship as a challenge to overcome and even as a new entrepreneurial quest. It's this spirit that gets them through it all. Jim's story is one that is both an inspiration and a reminder that we entrepreneurs are resilient and that we can—and in many cases must—defy the odds.

—Ken

When faced with challenges, people often say, "When it rains, it pours." I've always welcomed challenges and have an ability to weather most storms. When I left the Thunderbird School of Global Management, MBA in hand, I felt ready for battle. But a personal tsunami soon interrupted my forecast of glorious days on the business battlefront.

After running my successful start-up for three years, I decided to go for hypergrowth by franchising my homeowners' association property management business, Parker Finch Management. The business had posted consistent but unexciting profits, and I decided that now was the time to swing for the fences. It would be a challenge, but I was more than ready for it.

The list of tasks required was daunting, and I followed the textbook formula. I added seasoned franchise talent to my team. I recruited the head of franchise sales from a 1,000-location company. I raised capital to pay for expanding the business infrastructure to support our upcoming volume of business. And I invested in all the legal paperwork such as franchise offering documents and agreements to expand the franchise nationally under U.S. and state laws.

About a year into the ramp-up, we'd sold only four franchises and spent well over $1,000,000. The pipeline of prospects inquiring about buying one of our franchises grew, but almost none of the inquiries made it to a closed deal. Much-needed revenue became more and more elusive. What was the problem? I took the question as a challenge to solve, and I began to work even harder, analyzing and deconstructing our franchise offering in the hopes of finding out why so few of our prospects were completing the purchase.

Long days of endless meetings meant my "real work" had to wait until everyone else had gone home for the day. Consulting with managers, advisors, and mentors took up the better part of my eight hours. I worked the franchise and the numbers well into the evening to keep the business moving forward. But still, it was a mystery. How could such a successful stand-alone business model fail to franchise successfully? The seasoned experts said the same thing: "Your analysis of the marketplace and the industry is great. Your price point is right on. Your prototype franchise has proven the model." And yet, there was no onslaught of takers.

I've always had a strong work ethic, so working harder seemed the like the natural solution. I remembered all those case studies from school, the "success stories" about the founders of Yahoo! who worked so much in the beginning that they actually slept under their desks at their office. I had no problem with floors, if that's what it took to be successful. No pain, no gain, right?

On top of working continually, my commute was an hour and a half each day, so I tried to squeeze in more work while I was stuck in the car by calling each of my managers to ask for daily reports. My entrepreneurial dream and venture were challenging for sure, more challenging than I'd believed possible. But I was determined to make it work. I saw the potential and the promise. A challenge wasn't going to get in my way.

Of course, all this extra effort took a toll on me personally. I had little time for my family, but my wife, Audra, and I believed strongly in the business. We made building it my number one priority. We were both willing to sacrifice a little now for a better life tomorrow. Never did I ever expect that the biggest challenge of my life was about to begin.

The Real Challenge

My two-year-old daughter was definitely going through her "terrible twos" and my three-month-old was just starting to sleep four hours in a row. My wife carried most of the burden of raising our children. Sure, I missed spending time with them, but I told Audra that if I worked hard now while the kids were so young, by the time they were old enough to miss me, we'd be rich and I'd hang out with them all the time. Operating on no sleep, she smiled patiently.

Meanwhile, Parker Finch was continuing to burn through the cash we'd raised. Our burn rate was far faster than our incoming revenue, and the stress only increased with every passing day. I had not only my family to consider in all of this, but my investors, too. What a shock! My venture was supposed to be like Yahoo!, not failing, but in retrospect, what I was going through was nothing.

In July, I went away on an annual week-long business trip. I talked to Audra on the phone a couple of times that week, and she seemed to be a bit distracted. "Who wouldn't be," I thought. She was juggling our two kids, the house, and all her other responsibilities managing our household. On the phone, after a brief conversation, I told her, "I love you. We'll take some time and catch up when I get home this weekend."

That week away was eventful, giving me insight into my goals, my business, and my cash flow challenges. It was also eventful for Audra and my daughter. While I was away, my wife had her cousin, a leading expert in speech therapy, evaluate Sophia. Audra's mom had connected them because she intuitively knew that Sophia was not talking or behaving like other two-year-olds.

Audra watched the evaluation unfold. Sophia was asked to play with toys, asked her name, asked where her mommy was, and asked to follow directions. Instead of responding to the requests, she ran around the room touching everything like a beautiful butterfly, as if no one was with her, as if no demands at all were asked of her. My wife watched it all quietly, and within minutes everything became perfectly and painfully clear for her. I, on the other hand, would be pained by a slow realization.

Aware that this was not the stuff of a phone conversation, Audra didn't tell me about the evaluation until I got home. During the conversation, I told Audra that Sophia was just going through a stage. I told her that having a newborn in the house had made my wife sleep deprived. "This is nothing," I said. "Perhaps things will be better after we both get some rest."

Audra wasn't convinced, and she pulled some strings to get us in to see a pediatric behavioral specialist who had a six-month waiting list in just a couple weeks. He must be good, I thought, but I was still surprised at the demand for his specialty. Little did I know why there was such a long list.

A couple weeks later, on the heels of another marketing meeting to unravel my business mystery, I ran out of my office so that I could meet my wife at the doctor's office. The doctor observed Sophia playing with some toys. When he tried to talk to her unsuccessfully, I explained that Sophia didn't talk much to strangers. He smiled politely.

> *I've always had a strong work ethic, so working harder seemed the like the natural solution.*
>
> *I remembered all those case studies from school, the "success stories" about the founders of Yahoo! who worked so much in the beginning that they actually slept under their desks at their office.*

By the end of the appointment the doctor told us exactly what we didn't want to hear. We wanted to hear that Sophia was just a headstrong two-year-old and not to worry, that before long we wouldn't be able to keep her quiet and that we'd be wishing for the days when she seemed like she was in her own world. But that's not what he said. He said, "Sophia has Pervasive Development Disorder–Not Otherwise Specified (PDD-NOS)."

"What does that mean exactly?" I asked.

The doctor looked at us over the top of his glasses, and said, "Sophia's young, so catching it this early is good. If she were a little older, I'd say she has autism."

"Autism?" I felt numb. He told us that there were a couple of books that we could buy from his receptionist and that we should consider changing what Sophia ate. I barely heard what he said. It was as if someone had punched me in the gut. I was caught off guard. Autism? I didn't know much about it, but it didn't sound good.

We were in a state of shock as we paid the receptionist and took our two autism books to the car, pulling Sophia along by the hand.

We said nothing.

A New Reality

I returned to my office in a blur. I had a long list of meetings ahead of me that day and still needed to figure out how to stop the company from losing money. The demands on me at work had no end in sight and now we had this new challenge. I was in shock and had no idea of the impact my daughter's PDD-NOS, autism, or whatever it was, would have on my life. It took a couple of days for me to realize that Sophia's diagnosis wasn't a challenge like any I'd experienced before. Instead, it was a life-changing tsunami that poured over my family and kept us gasping for air on a daily basis.

The following Monday afternoon, I held a meeting with my management team. Struggling to hold back my tears, I explained to them that my oldest daughter was just diagnosed with autism and that I would be cutting back on my time at the office. I paused several times to regain what composure I had left. I said, "The company's success is in your hands. I won't be in the office for a couple of weeks while I research how to help my daughter." I'd had challenges before, and I only knew one way to respond: Work harder. "Find the solution," I said to myself. "Be the problem-solver this time when you need it most." One thing the doctor had forgotten to tell us is that there's no known treatment for PDD-NOS. No recovery. No cure. No hope?

Work Harder

After several weeks of spending my days (and nights) learning about autism and the potential new treatments that were in various stages of development, I learned that about one in ninety children are diagnosed with autism. I also learned that one in 100,000 kids with autism were "recovering" from this illness. No wonder our behavioral specialist had such a waiting list.

Yes, the numbers sounded daunting, but to me they said that there was some chance of helping my precious Sophia. I begin attending a few meetings back at the office. The surprising news was that the company hadn't gotten any worse in my absence. Unfortunately, it hadn't gotten any better, either.

I decided that given an unknown future of medical costs and caregiver expenses, the business was no longer a place where I worked, but instead a strategic asset to be used as a vehicle to fund Sophia's medical expenses.

I posted a sign above the inside of my office door so that I could see it while I was working at my desk. It read: "Defy the Odds." That was my goal with my business. I needed my business to defy the odds so that it could support my mission of curing my daughter's illness—and defy the odds of autism.

At the same time, it became clear that the franchising effort was a failure. Several franchise consultants touted it as the "best concept developed in a long time," and a few franchise lawyers even said it was a better business model than any of their other clients' (not that they would admit that to their paying customers).

Now knowing that my business was a means to the end of helping my daughter, I attacked it like a hungry lion staring at a raw T-bone steak. I cut costs immediately. I stopped the coffee service. I ended the free snacks in the company kitchen. I laid-off interns and support staff. I stopped spending cash on franchise marketing and advertising. I put everyone on variable compensation plans.

I made a difficult decision to break a multiple-year lease on downsize office space. I stopped paying for the company's management team perks. I renegotiated each and every vendor contract to get payments deferred and interest rates reduced. Nothing was sacred except, of course, my daughter.

Meanwhile, back at home, things continued to get worse with Sophia. She developed a blank stare and would no longer talk or even smile. She looked like she was trapped in a shell the shape of a two-year-old child's body. It was heart-wrenching.

To learn about autism faster, I decided to start attending autism conferences around the country, which required me to be away from work more and more. Without a large management team to rely on, I prioritized everything. Most of the things I used to labor over didn't even make the list now. No longer did I work late at the office, unless I was researching autism treatments on the Internet while I waited out rush-hour traffic.

Audra worked tirelessly to get services and therapists for Sophia. She secured appointments in weeks that took less aggressive parents months to get. We quickly had Sophia doing forty hours a week of behavioral therapy in our home. Audra also drove Sophia to speech therapy, occupational therapy, music therapy, and physical therapy each week.

I knew that anything ending in the word "therapy" couldn't be cheap, so I continued to squeeze more and more profit out of the business. The streamlined business processes and procedure manuals that we originally built for franchisees were actually making our original business (the franchise prototype) even more profitable. At last, we were realizing a benefit from all of that early hard work. We started seeing some black instead of only red on the income statement.

Taking my company through a turnaround while navigating the family crisis of my daughter's illness made me laser-focused on my company's reason for existing. There was no doubt. I was in business to make profit. Businesses exist to make a profit. And not to profit some day in the distant future—to make profit now.

A New Beginning

Today, I have a company president running the day-to-day operations of Parker Finch Management. I pay him based on a percent of the company's profit. Each Monday, I go into the office to sign checks, review financial reports, and discuss sales and marketing with the team. My dedicated office and desk are history. I just boot up my laptop in the office's conference room for the few hours a week that I'm there.

Sophia's making slow but gradual progress, and we continue to fill her schedule with therapists and are trying new treatments on a regular basis. I was right about the medical bills. Many of the therapies and treatments that have helped our daughter make so much progress are not covered by insurance. We've shouldered the financial burden, as do so many families caring for children with autism.

Now that we have settled into the realities and the routines of our life, Audra and I have time to give back to the community. We started a 501 (c) (3) charity called Prevent Autism Today (www.PreventAutism.org). Its mission is to eliminate all new cases of autism in the U.S. by January 1, 2020. There are too many parents drowning in the challenging waves of autism that crash down on their families.

Often, out of the most dire of circumstances, we find our life's mission. That's true for Audra and me. Now, my challenge isn't just to grow a company for the freedom that wealth can bring; it's to fulfill both my family and my entrepreneurial dreams while I continue the quest to protect other families from the nightmare

Audra and I have lived through for the last five years.

Autism is an epidemic in the U.S., and I'm setting out to prove it doesn't have to be. Thanks to the gift of Sophia, I now see my purpose is to prevent autism today. My purpose is to defy the odds.

 James Small is a successful business owner, real estate investor, entrepreneur, consultant, and philanthropist. Prior to launching his own consulting practice, James built the nation's first franchise in the field of community association management. He leveraged the principles of business systems and private equity to rapidly grow a business from his spare bedroom into one of the best-known brands in a $12 billion industry in just three years. James has been awarded the distinguished Thirty-Five Under 35 honor given to up-and-coming executives in Arizona and the Forty Under 40 award for being one of his state's top leaders in business and community service. He is also the founder of a 501 (c)(3) charity called Prevent Autism Today.

Afterword

I hope this book has inspired you, not just to begin your journey toward being a self-employed entrepreneur but also toward understanding that by doing so you will become part of the solution to so much that is wrong with our economy and the world.

In this book, the authors bare their souls and show their individual humility in sharing valuable lessons, and each shares personal stories and experiences that many people would look at as failures. These men and women, pioneers at their very core, want you to succeed. They want you to experience financial freedom and to know that you can create something from nothing, and do it again and again. And that's true power. Not the power a politician or a middle manager seeks, but instead, the power to control your own destiny by having the confidence and experience to earn your way with just another idea.

I want to encourage you to take the bold step of taking control of your life and your future by using your time and talents to create your own opportunities. You can do it.

And as you read these stories, I hope you notice the very common theme of passion. Money should never be your sole motivator. To find true wealth and happiness you must uncover your gifts and passions and link them to the practical needs of the world. Find work you like, and the money will follow. Work for the fun of it, and the money will arrive.

The majority of the people think that separating their work from their passion is what they're supposed to do, and in turn they prefer a higher paycheck to higher happiness. That mistake can cost you your soul. I can also assure you that high compensation and high happiness are not correlated. They have nothing to do with each other.

If you're happy in what you're doing, you'll like yourself, you'll have inner peace, and you'll be more confident. And if you have that, along with physical health, you'll have more success than you can possibly imagine. What we think or what we believe is, in the end, of little consequence. The only thing of consequence is what we do.

I encourage you to come back and reread these stories when you need a little inspiration. In the trenches of entrepreneurship it's easy to get down and feel defeated. Sometimes all you need is a little reminder that men and women have gone before you and have succeeded, facing the same or even greater challenges than you're facing. Take courage and comfort in these stories, time and again.

Support Small Business

If you're not ready to jump out and start your own business (though I hope you are), I hope this book has shown you the importance of the small business person and given you a passion to support small businesses and entrepreneurs.

Recently, I had the opportunity to host a wonderful event at my home. As part of a combined program with EO and the U.S. State Department, a group of us dined with young entrepreneurs and business owners from Yemen, Tunisia, Niger, Brunei, Trinidad, and Tobago.

As we rounded the table sharing various conversations and experiences, it became very clear to me that the most important issues for small business and entrepreneurs are universally the same across the planet, and the most balanced economies are those that politically support the small businessperson and the entrepreneur. A successful community is one that fosters new ideas, products and services.

Every country and every city in the world has entrepreneurs and small business, and it's these people and businesses that are creative and willing to take risks with their own money. But not all politicians are at the forefront of encouraging these businesses to succeed. However, if you look at who really supports local communities, physically and financially, you'll see it's the small businesses. Political leaders need to know that a successful economic system is one that provides incentives that encourage small businesses which in turn will create jobs and generate a more diverse tax base for that community.

Beyond creating jobs and generating tax revenue, small businesses are essential to the social fabric of towns and cities, and they foster a sense of community. Small businesses support local civic initiatives and open their doors and wallets to charitable events. The businessperson helps the local community by running a successful business, and local economy is being directly stimulated by its actions.

To emphasize my point on the business impact in a community, you need to look no further than Massachusetts Institute of Technology's (MIT) Entrepreneur program offered through its business school.

Today, if the companies founded by MIT graduates formed an independent nation, their revenues would comprise the seventeenth-largest economy in the world—and a conservative estimate of their annual sales would equal $2 trillion.

The MIT $100,000 competition alone has given birth to over 85 companies over the past 20 years. Together, they've attracted $600 million in venture capital funding. As Lesa Mitchell, a vice president of the Kauffman Foundation, explains, "MIT's significant economic impact is of particular interest because it provides an important model for universities interested in helping their students become more effective entrepreneurs."

And the state that benefits most from these successful programs? Massachusetts, of course, with over one million jobs created from over 6,900 MIT alumni companies.

Entrepreneurs are vital to economic growth, and because of this, legislators and other leaders who create economic policies should strive to encourage the innovation and risk taking of entrepreneurs.

While many of the big corporations wait for bailouts, small businesses remain essential to the nation's economic well being. Independent business owners are the ones most at risk of failure because, unlike large corporations, they have fewer cost-trimming options. And when it comes to financing or lines of credit, they haven't received the attention or the money the government has lavished on big business.

There is still much to do. For the U.S. to remain a leader in innovation, supporting small businesses and entrepreneurs is essential. It's important that we understand and support this New Business Class, the entrepreneur and the small business, because they are the lifeblood of our new economy. I encourage you to be aware of these issues and to write your congressional representatives and your senators to ask them to support policies that support small businesses.

Last Thought

As we come to the end of this book, I want to share one last thought. One thing I've learned from the school of hard knocks is that you can't move toward the future without turning the page on the past.

If you want to move forward in your life, personally or professionally, whether you're an entrepreneur or not, you need to make mentoring or coaching a regular part of your practice. I realized this early on in life and continue to seek guidance from coaches and mentors on numerous issues.

People seldom improve when they have no other model but themselves or their surrounding circle of influence as a reference. Most people have gone further than they thought they could because someone else pushed them, and I can tell you from experience: Few things in the world are more powerful than a positive push.

Unlike friends in your life, a mentor or a coach will tell you the truth about yourself. Some people can handle this and others cannot. A mentor or a coach can provide you with an objective view of yourself and your life. The feedback you get is invaluable information, should you choose to accept it. I can promise you that if you do accept it, it will change your life.

To find a coach or mentor on your own, you only need to identify someone you admire and respect. It could be anyone. Best of all, it doesn't need to cost you anything but some time and some initiative. There is a wealth of experience literally right in front of you; you just need to know where to look. Life is full of lessons, if you have the courage to ask questions.

On my website, thesleepinggiant.com, I have some detailed information and questions for helping you to find and then ultimately select a coach or mentor. In a world full of adversity and uncertainty, it's always comforting to know that there's someone—whether it's a friend, a family member, or a coach—to give you a helping hand.

Trust me on this: If you take action right now and find a coach or a mentor, this one change will improve your quality of life and your future.

With a book like this, inspiration comes easy. After all, these stories are inspiring and motivating. But inevitably, you come to the end of the book and are faced with the question, "Now what?"

So, I thought it would be a good idea to include some valuable resources that will help you as you begin your entrepreneurial journey.

Best of luck, and Godspeed.

Websites

Entrepreneurship.org – The Kauffman Foundation runs this site, which features hundreds of how-to articles for entrepreneurs.

EOnetwork.org – The Entrepreneurs' Organization's official website showcases this peer-to-peer network that enables entrepreneurs to learn and grow from each other, leading to greater business success and an enriched personal life.

Entrepreneur.com – the website for Entrepreneur Magazine which is a great resource for a free newsletter, multiple stories & ideas.

Business.gov – The central source for federal, state, and local information for businesses; learn about employment laws, where to apply for government grants and loans, and more.

BizStats.com – Free statistics and financial ratios for businesses by industry; find out what the average firm in your industry spends and earns.

BusinessFinance.com – This lender-matching service offers a range of useful information on various ways to finance a business.

Nielsen.com – Snapshots of consumer trends in different markets, from groceries to movies, by one of the oldest and biggest market-research firms.

Access eCommerce Guide – Even internet-illiterate entrepreneurs can learn almost everything they need to start an e-commerce business here.

Small Business Development Center (SBDC) – SBDCs are sponsored by the Small Business Association.Most services are free. Check out sba.gov/sbdc.

Small Business Advancement National Center (sbaer.uca.edu) – The nation's researchers contribute to this trove of scholarly articles on small-business issues.

Small Business School (smallbusinessschool.org) – View online videos and read transcripts of presentations on financing.

Statistical Abstract of the US (www.census.gov/compendia/statab) – The US Census Bureau's comprehensive and authoritative rundown of statistics on America's economy and society.

Blogs

thesleepinggiant.com
A free website that supports the entrepreneurial community.

paulgraham.com
Paul Graham is the founder of Viaweb, His essays are some of the best articles on startups and entrepreneurship ever and should be on the reading list of every aspiring entrepreneur.

mixergy.com
Mixergy is a blog by Andrew Warner, a successful entrepreneur. The blog has a collection of interviews with a lot of startup and more about their early startup days and their experiences.

steveblank.com
A blog on startups by Steve Blank, a serial entrepreneur turned professor who taught a course on entrepreneurship to students at U.C. Berkeley and Stanford University. Excellent advice for new startups.

cdixon.com
The blog of Chris Dixon, the co-founder of Hunch and an early investor in many successful startups like Skype, Foursquare, Stack Overflow, TrialPay, DocVerse, and Invite Media.

startuplessonslearned.com
A startup blog by Eric Ries, a proponent of the Lean Startup Methodology.

blog.asmartbear.com
A startup blog by Jason Cohen, a successful entrepreneur who founded Smart Bear Software.

mashable.com
Mashable is a tech news blog that covers web and social media startups.

About the Author

Married to an Entrepreneur...
by Laura McElroy

My roller coaster ride started seventeen years ago when I met Ken. At the time, I was a very new Registered Nurse and had a new job in a hospital. I was young and naïve and excited to have a "safe and secure job." I had barely heard the word entrepreneur, and really did not know what it meant. Early on, the years were very lean, with me supporting us on a nurse's salary. Other years have been good, financially, but it can sometimes be a strain on our family due to travel, work hours, etc...

Ken's entrepreneurial spirit has rubbed off over the years, enabling me to have a part-time business that is flexible around our kids' schedules. It's shown me what freedom really means. Freedom to pursue a passion and love what you do every day! I have also learned that the everyday challenges are just that: challenges. You take the highs and the lows... like a roller coaster ride. Appreciate the highs and hang on during the lows—or you can scream with your hands up in the air as you roll down hill. I've done both!

Mentor to an Entrepreneur...
by Charlie Dunlap

Ken McElroy is an exceptional human being. I know him as a captivating, warm and friendly man who is equally comfortable with the heads of industry or the young boy down the street. He combines common sense and humility with tremendous energy and intellect. What you see in Ken is what you get...no masks or agendas, just an amazingly capable, thoughtful and generous man, whose family comes first. Over the years, our times spent together have been invigorating for me. I often leave those times together having received more from Ken than I've given.

Son of an Entrepreneur...
by Kyle McElroy • Age 12

Last summer my little brother and I started our own business! We would go out onto the golf course after it closed and find golf balls. We would clean them up and sell them back to the golfers for about $1 a piece. (Pro Vs were 3 for $5 and a dozen for $20 because they are better balls). It was one of the best summers of my life. By the end we actually had orders for a certain type of ball in large quantities. This one lady that lived just down the street from me ordered 50 Callaway's. During that summer we had made a little over $500! But that is only one way my Dad has inspired me to have my own business...I mean, be an entrepreneur.

Son of an Entrepreneur...
by Kade McElroy • Age 9

We are able to take lots of vacations, like Australia, New Zealand, Mexico, Canada and Hawaii. Our golf ball business this summer made me over $250, we even brought in some other kids as partners and they made money, too. I like having my own money so I can spend some of it if I want to... like a new skateboard. Using some of the golf ball money, we just started our next business, making and selling duct tape wallets for $10 each to other kids.

Mother of an Entrepreneur...
by Mary McElroy

We are so proud of Ken, as an entrepreneur in the business world. He understands the sense of fulfillment you receive when you lend a hand, as he has done, in so many areas. Ken's father and I have always felt it imperative to really listen to your children. Let them experience the world at their own speed, get their feet wet...but always let them know you are there for them in good and bad times.

Other Books
by Ken McElroy

The ABC's of Real Estate Investing

The Advanced Guide to Real Estate Investing

The ABC's of Property Management

He is also a contributor to
The Real Book of Real Estate

EO | Entrepreneurs'
Organization

*fueling the
entrepreneurial engine*

The Entrepreneurs' Organization (EO)

As the world's most influential community of entrepreneurs, the Entrepreneurs' Organization (EO) is an innovative support system for today's business owners. Since 1987, EO has served as a global thought leader on entrepreneurship, enriching members' lives through dynamic peer-to-peer learning, once-in-a-lifetime experiences and connections to experts. A non-profit organization, EO wields a powerful influence in the lives of 7,500 members across 118 chapters in 38 countries. EO members are some of the most successful business owners in the world, generating a combined US$124 billion in annual revenue.

EO also supports the growth of emerging entrepreneurs through its Accelerator program and the Global Student Entrepreneur Awards (GSEA). Accelerator is an education-based program designed to accelerate the financial goals of first-stage business owners. In a series of quarterly, high-impact learning events, the program provides entrepreneurs with the tools, knowledge and skills they need to generate more than US$1 million in annual revenue. In 2009, more than 200 entrepreneurs participated in Accelerator, of which 11 percent reached their revenue goal. Considering only four percent of all startups ever reach the million-dollar milestone, the success rate of Accelerator speaks to the strength of the program. Participants credit the tools, learning and connections made through Accelerator for helping them grow their business.

Similarly, the GSEA is the premier award program for undergraduate students that own and run businesses while attending college or university. Designed to recognize, celebrate and encourage today's "Sleeping Giants," GSEA operates as an international series of competitions allowing entrepreneurs to compete against their global peers. Through GSEA, budding entrepreneurs are afforded new avenues of growth, receive substantial visibility and are rewarded for having innovative, profitable and socially responsible companies. Hundreds of student entrepreneurs have found success through the GSEA program, and many have gone on to become global business leaders.

Mentorship programs like Accelerator and GSEA equip entrepreneurs with the knowledge and experience they need to become giants of business and community. These programs are in service of beginner and experienced entrepreneurs, and they reflect EO's desire to stimulate the economy, foster job growth and encourage entrepreneurship in all corners of the world. It is this commitment to entrepreneurial growth that helps EO build a better tomorrow, today.

To learn more about the Entrepreneurs' Organization, visit www.eonetwork.org. To learn more about Accelerator and GSEA, visit http://accelerator.eonetwork.org and www.gsea.org.

NOTES

NOTES